Learning
for Leadership

A Facilitative Approach for Training Leaders

Yael Hellman, EdD

ASTD
PRESS

ASTD Press is an internationally renowned source of insightful and practical information on workplace learning, training, and professional development.

ASTD Press
1640 King Street Box 1443
Alexandria, VA 22313-1443 USA

Ordering information: Books published by ASTD Press can be purchased by visiting ASTD's website at store.astd.org or by calling 800.628.2783 or 703.683.8100.

Library of Congress Control Number: 2014934632

ISBN-10: 1-56286-899-3
ISBN-13: 978-1-56286-899-4
e-ISBN: 978-1-60728-408-6

ASTD Press Editorial Staff:
Director: Glenn Saltzman
Manager and Editor, ASTD Press: Sarah Cough
Community of Practice Manager, Human Capital: Juana Llorens
Editorial Assistant: Ashley Slade
Cover Design: Bey Bello
Text Design: Marisa Kelly

Printed by Versa Press, Inc., East Peoria, IL, www.versapress.com

Dedication

To my leadership role model, Bryce D. Hellman.

Contents

Acknowledgments

I am grateful to the many friends, colleagues, family members, and past and present students who contributed directly and indirectly to this book. I offer special thanks to Dr. Alisa Reich, my personal editor, career coach, and cheerleader.

I would also like to acknowledge ASTD's Juana Llorens for making this project a reality and my editor, Sarah Cough, for enhancing it. Reinhardt Schuerger helped me navigate the complexities of law enforcement, and Steven Zipperman opened doors to the police department and its leadership academy. Finally, I appreciate the Los Angeles County Sheriff's Department for its support of ground-breaking leadership development programs. The generous efforts of all let me build something far bigger than I could have done alone.

Introduction

As a teacher of adults, I respect their life knowledge, varied abilities, and learning preferences, and allow them the greatest possible freedom to educate themselves. This respect—the heart of adult education—encourages the reflection and emotional intelligence I value most in mature learners. So I don't operate as a traditional professor—turning my back to trainees and lecturing at them. Instead, I create a participant-centered group environment that feels so safe that it can contain and ignite individuals' unique energies and openness to experience.

While some trainees—and trainers—find participant-led interactive instruction foolish or frightening at first, decades of research and teaching have proven that this approach best develops deep, lasting leadership skills through immediate, hands-on practice. In fact, I discovered that the group you'd expect to be the most resistant to facilitation—authority-oriented, toughened police officers in a paramilitary organizational culture—embrace this environment and grow tremendously as leaders within it.

This manual grew out of my years training leaders in academic and other settings. It culls the very best practices and resources, offers tried-and-true lesson outlines, and presents real-life accounts of the pitfalls and potentials of facilitation. These practical instructions and "trade secrets" explain and illustrate the adult education, group dynamics, and leadership information presented here.

Of course, even with the best tips, it takes practice to meet the intellectual and emotional demands of teaching a participant-centered group. I'm confident that applying the educational theory and techniques in this book, and witnessing your trainees experiencing them, will show you why and how facilitation creates profound, practical executive wisdom. Most important, it will strengthen your powers of leadership development.

To master and enjoy that goal, recall the basic rule of the facilitative approach: Know yourself, and know your trainees. Only then will you see when to lead and when to follow, and be able to transform learners into leaders.

PART I

THEORIES OF LEADERSHIP TRAINING

Chapter 1

Learning Leadership

This chapter will cover:

- findings about workplace learning
- educational theory terminology
- why adults learn best through interactive instruction
- major adult instructional approaches and the advantages of the facilitative approach
- trainee views of the pitfalls and promise of facilitative instruction.

DEVELOPMENTAL LEARNING THEORY

Great educators have long known that children's learning capacities and motivations differ from those of adults, and grow just as their bodies do. Medieval rabbis traced letters in honey to draw four-year-olds to study, and Enlightenment thinker Jean-Jacques Rousseau preached gentle, natural socialization of the young in *Émile, or On Education*. Piaget, Erikson, and Vygotsky keenly observed the intellectual and emotional stages children attain as they mature. Contemporary learning studies confirm these earlier testimonies to the gradual evolution of children's cognitive, personal, and social skills.

But it's only relatively recently that researchers have recognized similar maturation in adult learning abilities and motivators, and have come to see these as continuing to evolve throughout life. Scholars such as Arlin, Gruber, Merriam, and Caffarella have suggested a fully mature stage of cognitive development that follows Piaget's developmental stages: creative problem-solving. Further studies have transformed adult learning theory into a field in its own right, defined by the National Research and Development Centre (2010) as "the entire range of formal . . . and informal learning activities which are undertaken by adults after a break since leaving initial education and training, and which results in the acquisition of new knowledge and skills."

Not surprisingly, adult learning theory expanded with the burgeoning of adult education programs in colleges and universities and of leadership training in almost every business and public sector organization. As early as 1972 Ruyle and Geiselman noted a survey by University of California, Berkeley's Center for Research and Development in Higher Education, which showed that roughly 1,400 two- and four-year institutions offered "nontraditional" degree programs to working adults, and Finch and Rahim found that 7 percent of those programs were already more than 10 years old. Practically oriented executive training in private businesses and public sector organizations has been around even longer.

HOW KNOWING ADULT LEARNING THEORY HELPS YOU TRAIN LEADERS

Despite the seeming universality of adult training programs, theorists define adult learning very differently. This variance comes both from advances in the field of cognitive neuroscience and from the researchers' own methods and philosophies, ranging from humanism to personal responsibility orientation to behaviorism to critical perspectives and beyond.

But understanding these different contributions of adult learning theorists isn't just academic. It gives you, as a leadership educator, a concrete grasp of which methods and activities will work and which won't—and why—in your training of future executives and top-line managers. As one rather hard-boiled alum I taught wrote in a course evaluation, "I paid you money to teach me. Not cuddle me. You came through and taught me about group dynamics and real leadership. It was a little confusing, but the dividend was far greater. Thank you."

We'll see later in this chapter that the facilitative approach blends the very best of many teaching philosophies and techniques. But now we need to look at each of those elements separately.

Adult Learning Theories

By the middle of the last century, Knowles (1970) contributed to the adult learning field by popularizing the term *andragogy* (teaching men, as contrasted with *pedagogy*, teaching children) and defining it as "the art and science of helping adults learn." He based his practice on five essential qualities he identified in people:

- Self-Concept: Mature people advance in self-knowledge and self-direction.
- Experience: Adults draw on their experiences to aid learning.
- Readiness: Adults' openness to education matches the social roles they've mastered.
- Orientation: Adults want to apply new knowledge immediately to solve problems.
- Motivation: As people mature, their motivation to learn is increasingly internal.

Knowles argued that adults must participate directly in planning and evaluating their instruction. Their active experience—including mistakes—should form the basis for learning, as should a focus on subjects immediately relevant to their work or private life. In short, Knowles thought that adult learning is, and therefore adult instruction must be, personal and problem-centered, rather than content-oriented.

Collins (1994) specified that what makes adult learning *adult* is its inter-weaving of theory with application, so that learning prompts practice and practice prompts learning. Adults learn when the objectives seem realistic and relevant to them; when they initiate and control their own learning; when immediate experiences let them apply the learning at work; when classroom feedback supports them instead of judging them; when small-group activities provide chances to apply, analyze, synthesize, and evaluate material; when the diversity of their personal life experiences, skills, and interests are welcomed; and when coaching and follow-up help them perform and thus retain new skills. As one of my alums put it, "Our cohort was ideal because the students came from diverse professional backgrounds (private sector, engineering, law enforcement, education, health, etc.)."

Merriam and Caffarella (1999) broadened this appreciation of life experience to include not just personal history and skills, but also physical and psychological changes from aging. Biological and mental developments (including deterioration and diseases) and the new socio-cultural challenges they bring, impact an adult's performance and motivations for learning. This means each mature thinker brings several types of experience to class: life experience (including changes in cognitive abilities); work experience (including resulting habitual thought patterns); positive or negative learning experiences; gaps in educational history; and cognitive and physical factors affecting performance.

Argote, McEvily, and Reagans (2003) furthered Merriam and Caffarella's sensitivity to the many factors impacting adult learning by arguing that experience plays a role in one's ability to create, retain, and transfer knowledge. For them, older thinkers are characterized less by age than by learning traits: self-motivation and self-direction; capacity for group learning; curiosity; critical thinking skills; introspection; and the ability and desire to articulate and apply life experiences to course content. These aptitudes, Wynn (2006) warned, make teaching a classroom of mature learners both unique and challenging. For, while they share these strengths, they arrive from dissimilar backgrounds and bring varying levels of preparedness. Based on that, McCoy (2006) insisted that adult education be learner-centered, allowing participants to draw from their own lives, take responsibility for their learning, apply it immediately to real-life situations, and grow as self-directed and proactive learners.

Adult Learning Theory Consensus

Despite theoretical debates, then, most adult learning experts agree with the National Guidelines for Educating EMS Instructors that teachers of mature learners must first come to understand them, so they can guide them to know themselves as well as the course material. Equally, most adult education program planners should design courses with sensitivity to adult learning needs, as Caffarella (2002) counseled.

Researchers also concur that adults learn best when they desire to learn and are mentally ready for the challenge. To succeed, learners must first identify and own their goals, whether to improve work performance, family life, or health; enjoy the arts, physical recreation, or a hobby; or simply increase their knowledge. They must also collaborate with others, which means they must feel supported by, and must themselves support, class colleagues. Finally, mature learners have to participate actively in their education and in the assessment of their progress, and build on their own life wisdom.

To sum up, current learning studies suggest that adult learning techniques should parallel adults' cognitive and motivational qualities: life lessons, self-direction, readiness to work for individual goals, focus on real-life problem-solving, and the ability to cooperate for their own growth as well as that of an organization. This consensus shapes all major adult education approaches.

INSTRUCTIONAL APPROACHES USING ADULT LEARNING CHARACTERISTICS

We'll examine the primary techniques advocated by distinct adult learning theories—experiential, self-directed, transformational, group, and facilitative—because grasping their unique emphases lets you appreciate exactly what works in leadership development and why.

Experiential Learning

Experiential learning both uses learners' previous experience and creates new experiences in the classroom. It interweaves adults' personal-historical life knowledge with current hands-on classroom activities.

Perhaps the best reason to use experiential learning for adults, Candy (1991) suggested, is that hands-on learning appears to play an even greater role in adult education than in pedagogy, as mature persons seem to learn better through immediate experience. Adult education not only encourages older learners to experience actively in the classroom, but also to apply their new learning directly to job and life activities.

Like Dewey, Lewin, and Piaget, Kolb (1984) focused on students' cognitive development, though he gave greater weight to environmental and personal-historical forces. His learning model states that each of us prefers learning in a manner that is one of polar opposites: symbolic, intellectual conceptualization (abstract conceptualization), or sense-perception of the world (concrete experience). This choice usually suits our intellectual style, personality, and inborn or learned talents.

Those who know themselves best pick fields or careers that fit them best and in which they're most likely to succeed. Kolb, Boyatzis, and Mainemelis (2000) thought that "watchers" tend to favor reflective observation, while "doers" tend to favor active experimentation. For example, if two friends want to learn how to drive a car, one may choose to learn by observation and reflection—say, watching others drive and analyzing the DMV rules book. The other might just hop in behind the wheel and tool around in an empty parking lot!

But no matter how each friend chooses to start—with observation or concrete experimentation—both need to transform information in order to learn. Regardless of where one tends to enter the continuous spiral of education, everyone follows the same steps: Concrete experience creates observation and reflection, which give rise to new abstract concepts—new theories about the world—that are then tested by new concrete experience. More important, neither heredity nor training freezes the way we learn: We may freely choose to try new learning modes or to strengthen our less-used ones.

Action Learning

Emphasizing the value of experience in-the-now, in 2001 Stewart began presenting *action learning* by chiding that "classroom training is inefficient. Half the people in the room are secretly working on their 'real' jobs; half are so relieved not to be doing their real jobs, they've turned their minds entirely off. Half already know half the stuff being taught and are . . . [surfing the web] half will never need to know more than half of it." Like project-based education, learning teams, and learning coaching, action learning employs real organizational problems and group dynamics to learn, and is most widely used in managerial development.

Project-Based Learning

With *project-based learning*, participants work in groups to solve current problems. Learners gather information from a variety of sources, analyze and collate their information, and decide how to apply it. This approach connects class members to something real and activates their mature skills of collaboration and reflection. At the end, the learners themselves judge how much of the issue they captured and how well they communicated it. Note that the trainer's role throughout the process is to guide and advise, rather than to direct and manage, class members' work.

Critiques of Experiential Learning

Experiential learning theory has been censured for not taking into account cultural and individual differences that make the same classroom activity feel radically different to each person. For example, some may find a cooperative game silly and demeaning while others grasp the value of learning through a game. Or some may suffer paralyzing embarrassment from personal disclosure while others comfortably share their thoughts in public.

Perhaps more important for adults, experiential learning can overshadow the equally valid goal of mastering a subject. Even in active, project-based assignments, persons of different backgrounds and motivations may not see eye-to-eye, so more time and goodwill can be wasted in debating basic rules than in conquering course content.

Self-Directed Learning

When learning is *self-directed*, trainees take responsibility by first diagnosing personal educational needs and then setting goals, identifying resources, implementing strategies, and evaluating outcomes. Interestingly, proponents Marsick and Watkins (2001) claim that the power of this approach does not come from independent work itself, but rather from the value it places on incidental, or immediate, education. As far back as 1999, Rager calculated that over 95 percent of adults participated in some form of self-directed learning, during which they typically spent an average of 15 hours per week on a project.

Self-directed learning methods hinge on active learning. To understand that term as a developer of leaders, picture a continuum and put active learning at one end. What would you put at the opposite end—at passive learning? You would probably place lectures and other top-down, instructor-prepared presentations. And you'd be right: Research shows that after about 15 minutes of lectures or videos, most students find their attention wandering. So the passive learning these techniques embody seems—especially for adults—to be no learning at all.

The operative word in active learning, then, is learning, as Angelo and Cross (1993) clarified. And for those teaching executive skills, it's especially crucial to model effective communication, since nothing discourages loyalty (or learning) quicker than a "leader" (or teacher) who drones on without listening to, and learning from, those she or he is attempting to direct.

Critiques of Self-Directed Learning

One fundamental criticism of this approach is that, for both cognitive and emotional reasons, not all leadership learners can or wish to direct their own study. Even adults who seek to rise in an organization and who generally prefer independence may at times need formal, teacher-directed education because of the technical or novel nature of the subject. And psychologically, self-directed learning can feel so unstructured that learners get distracted from the material. As Merriam (2001) reminded us, many adults are unable or unwilling—especially at the start of a leadership training—to engage in self-directed learning because they lack confidence or know-how.

So it can be hypocritical to offer participants carte blanche to set course goals, formats, and assessment measures when they need to master new material and instructors need to hold them accountable for doing so. Finally, even if self-directed learning adequately explains how many individuals accrue knowledge, it sheds little light on how learning occurs in groups, and thus only weakly supports group training in leadership skills.

Transformational Learning

Transformational learning seeks far-reaching change within the learner, which Benson, Palin, Cooney, Farrell, and Clark all define as experiences that reshape the participant and produce a paradigm shift in thinking that affects all of his or her later experiences. As a developer of future leaders, you'll appreciate the centrality of this concept to your task. And as a leadership developer, the techniques and projects that help your trainees see themselves anew—and perhaps, actually change—will be the most powerful you can add to your teaching arsenal.

The transformational learning field emerged with the work of Mezirow, who developed the concepts of meaning schemes (separate chunks of a person's knowledge, values, and beliefs) and meaning perspectives (a person's overall worldview created by the collaboration of all of his or her meaning schemes). Our overarching meaning perspectives are acquired passively during childhood and youth. They work as perceptual filters—paradigms—that determine how we interpret every experience. Baumgartner and Taylor specified that meaning perspectives can be revealed by activities that test learners' values, beliefs, and decision-making process.

As Bennis and Thomas (2002) pointed out, meaning perspectives do evolve in response to emotionally powerful, life-changing events like divorce, death of a loved one, natural or man-made disasters, health crises, or financial ruin. Mezirow (1997) appreciated that people do not change their ideas willingly, as long as new information can somehow be squeezed to fit into their existing frame of reference. So the paradigm shifts needed for genuine transformative learning require the shock of cognitive dissonance—a massive clash between what we always thought and what we suddenly know. And for him, such shifts in paradigmatic meaning perspectives are the proper goal of transformational learning.

Mezirow identified three intertwining forces that unleash the mechanism of transformational learning in the classroom: experience, critical reflection, and rational discussion. Life experiences offer a starting point for transformational learning, but critical reflection is the distinguishing characteristic of adult learning and the best way mature thinkers can question the logic of their worldview. Rational discussion sparks change, as it forces participants to expose their meaning perspectives to others. Through this combination of self-questioning and communication, people can shift their paradigms to forge a more open and more accurate viewpoint. For Mezirow, the essential aim of transformational learning is the individual's developing greater autonomy as a person—Mezirow's defining criterion of maturity.

Imel (1998) noted that Boyd, another analyst of transformational learning, differed from Mezirow, believing that emotional experience, rather than rational discussion, causes change, and that such change leads not to autonomy, but to greater cooperation with, and compassion for, others. But for both thinkers, the core of transformational learning is its power, through sometimes painful realizations, to break down our unconscious, immature meaning perspectives and build truer, more open ones. Whichever slant makes more sense to you, as a trainer of future leaders you'll keep in mind that, rather than just imparting knowledge, you're actually guiding trainees to rethink, from the ground up, what they already "know" so they can be open to new insights.

Critiques of Transformational Learning

It's been argued that transformational theory judges learning very narrowly. First, Mezirow, at least, dismissed the role of non-intellectual, emotional experience in education. Second, identifying paradigm-altering awareness as the essence of learning is also limited: Not all education stems from a dramatic, earth-shattering personal paradigm shift, but rather from small adjustments to and enrichments of the thinker's understanding.

Group Learning

Group learning (perhaps ironically) relies first on the skill of the instructor to turn a random assortment of individuals into a working unit by empowering them to teach, govern, and evaluate themselves. Although all the approaches we examine in this chapter include group activities, group learning focuses primarily on group dynamics, and consciously aims to build a cooperative learning collective.

Like all teachers, group learning instructors maintain group members' focus and stoke constructive debate. They draw introverted people into discussions and protect them from brasher colleagues, rein in difficult participants, and provide content and sources to fuel research and debate.

But these instructors also try to remain neutral in the learning process, preferring that the collective guide and assess itself. Ideally, this neutrality frees them to concentrate on group dynamics so they can achieve the primary objective of group learning: bringing group members themselves to recognize, and repair, difficult group dynamics in order to maintain an effective learning environment.

Critiques of Group Learning

Many educators have noted that, while cooperation is undeniably valuable, participants in group learning courses often struggle to finish basic course tasks. And even when they successfully master group dynamics and the course subject, consistent learning from session to session, or with different subgroups of classmates, proves elusive.

Facilitation

To facilitate means to make some action or process easier. In general education, *facilitation* enables learners themselves to define and master course content.

But in leadership training specifically, facilitation does more than let the group teach itself material. It does what's infinitely harder and more rare: It makes participants actually practice leadership. By assigning learners as much control as possible over course aims, strategies, and evaluation, leadership facilitators instill leadership knowledge not only on an individual, intellectual level, but in a real-world field that's interactive, cooperative, and experiential.

Integrating Adult Education Approaches

Even more, facilitation uses the whole gamut of adult instructional approaches explored earlier in this chapter—experiential, self-directed, transformational, and group—and in a variety of learning modes, including verbal, visual, artistic, performance, individual, and collective. As one facilitative program graduate phrased it, it's "not a one-size-fits-all approach." By using all these techniques, it addresses learners simultaneously as individuals and as members of a community. More important, each strategy works to advance a single, but often elusive, goal: training lifelong learners to use their own initiative and ideas to solve problems as leaders, rather than to rely on authority—including the authority of the group.

Facilitation, then, helps learners find their own deep, flexible, and practical wisdom—exactly what you want your leadership trainees to discover and demonstrate. To achieve this end, the facilitative model exercises participants' personal motivations and cognitive strengths by placing them at the center of the learning experience. This self-directive role requires the group to craft its own decisions on course curriculum, session agendas, and assessment measures—and requires the facilitator to ensure that they are followed.

Techniques

Naturally, variations within the facilitative camp abound. Some practitioners cherish strict democracy while others prefer to direct, especially at the start.

Some prioritize mastery of the course subject, and some see group dynamics as the real subject, whatever the course description. But despite these nuances, Record (2004) found, facilitators agree that teachers and participants should dictate and deliver course content, objectives, methods, and evaluations of learning together, viewing and engaging group members as both a collective organization and as emerging executives.

Of course, good facilitators know that a group of individuals can't become an empowered whole without an early period of relying on the instructor. But instead of setting themselves up as authority figures, it is important that facilitators immediately create an atmosphere that encourages debate as well as the cooperation and the decisiveness—the leadership—of the whole class. The next chapters will show you, step by step, how you can craft this environment by first organizing class space and time to minimize barriers between yourself and trainees, set the stage for interactive learning, and schedule the learning session to maximize participation.

As a course progresses, effective facilitators show that they welcome not just differences of opinion but also differences of cognition, delivering information through a variety of verbal, non-verbal, auditory, visual, and kinesthetic techniques, which ensuing chapters will demonstrate. In brief, your aim—the aim of all great facilitators—is to gradually limit your interference, and to shift from acting as the authority to acting as a resource who introduces topics, mediates disputes, summarizes discussions, and points out sources of information.

Numerous scholars including Parks, Heifetz, Sinder, Jones, Hodge, Rowley, Johnstone, Fern, Kegan, and Lahey specify that participant-driven, experience-based facilitative techniques best engage participants emotionally and intellectually. Over years of implementing this advice I have refined fast-paced units that carry the action forward: icebreakers or warm-ups to focus learners on the session's agenda; interactive instruction to help them master content; group work, including collective projects; experiential exercises or games and joint activities that immediately apply new material; and wrap-ups to summarize one session and link it to an upcoming one. These activities teach and reinforce content by involving learners emotionally and physically in the process of setting and attaining collective goals, providing participants the experience of leadership long before they can claim the title. To illustrate from a course I delivered, one respondent to an after-course evaluation noted that "other schools only want you to write paper after paper and there is no real quality interaction and no real criticism." Another reflected that participants actually "had more 'power' than the instructors . . . to determine class content."

Critiques of Facilitation

Despite being widely recognized by public and private organizations as uniquely suited for leadership development, not every instructor can or wants to be a facilitator. Facilitative teaching can feel initially uncomfortable for trainers as well as for trainees. You'll find that some of the most determined raised hands belong to complainers: "This is OK for the others, but I already do this every day at work"; "We don't have time for games"; or "This sure is getting touchy-feely." Or you'll see slouching bodies, rolling eyes, tops of heads, or thumbs a-twitter on smartphones. Worse, very difficult participants (that is, non-participants) try to sabotage your lessons, wreck their subgroup's projects, or openly wrangle with colleagues.

In fact, trainees—and you—have good reason to resist facilitation: It's less predictable than a top-down, lecture-based course; makes participants and the instructor question their dearest assumptions and quarantine ingrained mental habits; exposes interpersonal relations and thus presses emotional buttons; and requires universal active participation. As a result, both learners and facilitators need to confront the natural human resistance to change—challenges that my longitudinal, cumulative, and multi-population study of facilitative training of leaders in the public sector (see Part II, chapter 5) pinpoints. Even more difficult, facilitative leadership training demands, from both teacher and participants, interconnection, introspection, trustworthiness, and ethical integrity.

But if you happen to value those intellectual, emotional, and moral capacities and believe—as I and most executive educators do—that they perfectly describe essential leadership qualities, choosing facilitation will richly reward you by enabling you to create confident, congenial, and principled leaders.

This book is designed to help you handle, utilize, and eventually even welcome any discomfort felt by you and your trainees along the way. Culled from years of facilitative leadership training, the following chapters and cases in point prove that, as the saying goes, "it happens to the best of us." That is, despite all your preparation, teaching talent, commitment to facilitation, and efforts to build a wonderful rapport with participants, you will experience failures and rebuffs. But take heart. And take advantage of the snares and saves that I've known, and you will emerge a far more effective (and happy) facilitator.

THE VALUE OF A FACILITATIVE APPROACH IN LEADERSHIP TRAINING

As suggested by its wide array of techniques, facilitation has an equally wide variety of purposes: instruction, cooperation, argumentation, consensus-building, performance, and reflection. And in addition to supporting the group's constant self-assessment, facilitators typically evaluate individual as well as collective assignments, projects, and research. In other words, facilitation integrates techniques from all the approaches discussed above, to meet mature leadership learners' central needs: individually relevant learning paths; appreciation of dynamics in the learning group and the groups they will eventually manage; and creative, transformative, practical learning.

How Facilitation Answers Critiques of Adult Learning Theory

One potent critique of adult learning theory in general is that people's learning modes may not remain stable over time. Research has found that adults over the age of 65 tend to become more observant and reflective. So not only do different students learn differently, but in various tasks and moods, the same person may learn differently.

Facilitation answers that fundamental criticism by agreeing with it! Precisely because mature leadership learners bring a host of differing—and evolving—skills and difficulties into the classroom, no single approach can work equally for each all the time. As a result, facilitation embraces all instructional strategies: verbal, kinetic, scholarly, artistic, creative, receptive, reflective, performative, argumentative, consensus-building, individual, and group. Most importantly, by blending all these approaches into a balanced whole, facilitation avoids the specific weaknesses of each individual approach in executive education.

In brief, by incorporating and counterweighing all of these adult instructional techniques, the inclusive approach of facilitation answers the basic critique leveled at each adult education approach equally—that adults do not all learn the same way, or the same way all the time.

Facilitation Closes the Divide Between Individuals and Organizations

In addition to weaving together techniques and insights on major adult educational approaches, facilitation resolves an apparent conflict in the adult learning field at the heart of leadership development. While all the theories recognize mature persons' cognitive and motivational qualities, their goals split rather neatly into two major camps: one that aims to educate and benefit the individual, and one that aims to educate and benefit the organization. By combining techniques—verbal and nonverbal, reflective and performative, research and creative, content-based and process-based, and individual and group—facilitation also integrates learner-focused and organization-focused education. Its knack for merging instructional modes, and for resolving individual versus group interests, makes facilitation an outstanding approach for leadership training.

Cognitive and Motivational Rationales for Facilitation

Supporting and energizing facilitation's learner-centered approach to training leaders is a wealth of findings that suggest lecturing actually limits learning in adults. You'll recall that Kolb (1984) explained the value of experience-based learning for mature participants by describing it as a spiral weaving together all the steps of knowledge: Experience fosters reflection; reflections coalesce into general concepts guiding future action; those later actions test the abstract concepts and, in turn, create new experiences. Miettinen (1998) and Raij (2007) added that such experience-based deep learning allows individuals' spontaneous feelings to mesh with their rational thinking in a new level of cognition. So, while information can be conveyed by lectures, self-education can't. Incorporating the intellectual and emotional elements of experiential learning theory, facilitation trains learners to lead by engaging their initiative and insight to solve adaptive challenges—problems demanding creative action rather than obedience to accepted views.

If lecturing appears to short-circuit adults' education, having them voice their own ideas seems to encourage deep learning. So facilitation purposefully develops language skills, based both on adult education theory and on solid research on the role of language itself as the creator of knowledge and action. Kegan and Lahey (2001) strongly suggest that our words not only express our feelings and thoughts, but to a great degree determine them, and so shape our behavior as well. In sum, mindful language, by sharpening the understanding and communication of our own experiences, encourages mindful action—the greatest lesson you can teach your executive trainees.

In this chapter, we've seen how facilitative leadership training lets instructors strengthen both the learning of leadership theory and, more difficult, its practice. By giving trainees plenty of control over course goals, methods, and evaluation, facilitators anchor leadership training on two fronts: the topic of leadership and the process of leading. In this way facilitators empower students to speak in, and listen to, their true voices. As an example of true self-direction, at the end of one leadership course I facilitated, the class spontaneously decided to name itself "La Familia Cohort" (the Cohort Family) and expressed their shared vision of themselves as leaders who "dream and aspire to grow intellectually, share knowledge, teach, challenge, respect each other, and ultimately graduate as a group/family."

Case in Point: Confronting Truth

The strongest proof of the transformational nature of facilitative learning I've ever seen happened spontaneously in a class of mine, and at the time it felt like its strongest disproof. At the next-to-last session of a year-long graduate degree program, in the middle of a class discussion, a trainee jumped up from his chair so quickly it clattered to the floor, and blurted out, "I don't want to be a leader! I don't know what I'm doing here." I thought the class would start laughing but they seemed to be in shock. For a second I felt like the biggest failure ever. But I walked over to him and asked him to sit down. Then I told him he was almost done with the program, and that just because he was studying leadership didn't mean he had to be a leader; he was learning how to be a team player and that was just as worthy. The trainee graduated, has kept in touch, and is doing well. Certainly, he was not cut out for the program he'd embarked on. But I see now that its reflective focus brought him to perhaps an even more valuable state of self-knowledge.

Organizational Rationale for Facilitative Leadership Training

Despite the universal popularity of private and public sector executive arts (leadership skills) training, organizations usually fail to change their internal behaviors. Jialin Yi (2005) attributes this lack of success to organizations' ignoring the characteristics of mature persons: "Within companies, instructional methods are designed for improving adult learners' knowledge and skills. It is important to distinguish the unique attributes of adult learners so as to be better able to incorporate the principles of adult learning in the design of instruction" (34). So using the principles of adult education in leadership training proves as crucial for helping institutions as it is for advancing individuals, because both organizations and adults progress when they apply learning directly to the workplace.

The methods Yi suggests to foster organizational change—problem-based learning to increase critical thinking skills; cooperative learning to build interpersonal communication; and situated learning to help participants acquire work-applicable skills and information—confirm the value of the multifaceted facilitative approach. The mix of active learning, sensitivity to group dynamics, and relevant course content supports not just the individual but the institution in which he or she works. And this is so because each of these aims follows the principles of adult learning theory: that mature learners bring and seek experience; can direct themselves; learn collaboratively; and want work-oriented growth.

As we noted, facilitative training of leaders requires the instructor to let group members both learn about leadership and actually lead. By fostering communication, cooperative, and executive skills, facilitation teaches trainees how to help the groups they'll manage in the future identify and achieve common goals—just as you will have done for them. Organizational theorist Parks (2005) noted that by training participants to express their ideas and to understand those of others, facilitation changes deeply ingrained mental habits and beliefs, and thereby lessens not only individuals' preconceptions, but entire organizations' resistance to growth. Its transformational power for individuals and for organizations makes facilitation especially valuable for leadership training.

SUMMARY

Adult learning theory supports the facilitative training of leaders. Educators of adults should recognize and utilize the mental and motivational qualities characterizing mature learners: diverse experience, self-directedness, the desire for real-life growth, and the ability to learn collaboratively. These intellectual and emotional traits have inspired a host of instructional approaches for this demographic, chief among them experiential, self-directed, transformational, group, and facilitation. The facilitative approach fuses all these methodologies, and thereby fills many of their shortfalls, including favoring one particular learning style or assuming that an adult's learning mode is fixed rather than dynamic.

In addition, facilitation meets goals in the field of adult learning theory that are usually seen as incompatible: individual and organizational transformation. Its ability to advance personal and organizational growth simultaneously demonstrates facilitation's special value for training leaders. We know creative problem-solving and communication skills are crucial for the advancement of individuals as well as business and public institutions. So facilitation, by giving a community of mature learners optimal control of their curriculum, class format, and evaluation, cultivates precisely the talents needed for them first to achieve, and later to instill, both personal and organizational excellence. One facilitative course alum found that "the program impacted my life in many ways. I am a stronger communicator and able to stand up for the ethics I believe in. I saw myself mature as a leader, developing stronger teamwork and understanding the difficulties and stages all of us must go through to accept changes in the workplace." Another learned with classmates to "improve ourselves and our department" by becoming "much better prepared to lead a group. I understand some of their thinking, concerns, wants, and needs."

In the next chapter, you'll learn the characteristics that make a classroom truly facilitative. We'll also look at techniques for creating a classroom environment that encourages active and interactive learning, as well as techniques for overcoming participant resistance.

REFLECTION AND NEXT STEPS

1. **Know yourself.** Are there aspects of facilitative training that make you nervous? Ones you're especially looking forward to? List these, and see if they follow a pattern or reveal a truth about you as an instructor.

2. **Reflect on this chapter.** How does understanding adult learning characteristics change—or confirm—your teaching style? How might insights from adult learning theory be especially relevant to teaching leadership?

3. **Recall the best course you ever took as an adult.** Using the elements of adult learning theory in this chapter, explain what made it successful and enjoyable.

4. **When you design your next course, use adult learning theory.** Practice explaining to reluctant trainees why you're asking them to follow certain rules or to do specific exercises, based on what you know about how mature learners grab and use information.

REFERENCES AND RESOURCES

American Heritage Dictionary of the English Language, 4th edition. (2006). Boston: Houghton Mifflin.

Angelo, T. and Cross, K.P. (1993). *Classroom Assessment Techniques*. San Francisco: John Wiley & Sons, Inc.

Argote, L., B. McEvily, and R. Reagans. (2003). "Managing Knowledge in Organizations: An Integrative Framework and Review of Emerging Themes." *Management Science*, 49: 571-582.

Arlin, P. (1984). "Adolescent and Adult Thought: A Structural Interpretation." In Commons, M., F. Richards, and C. Armon (editors), *Beyond Formal Operations: Late Adolescent and Adult Cognitive Development*. New York: Praeger.

Arlin, P. (1975). "Cognitive Development in Adulthood: A Fifth Stage." *Developmental Psychology*, 11:602-606.

Barkley, E. (2010). *Student Engagement Techniques: A Handbook for College Faculty.* San Francisco: Jossey-Bass.

Baumgartner, L. (2001). "An Update on Transformational Learning Theory." In Merriam, S. (editor), *The New Update on Adult Learning Theory: New Directions for Adult and Continuing Education.* San Francisco: Jossey-Bass.

Bennis, W., and R. Thomas. (2002). *Geeks and Geezers: How Era, Values, and Defining Moments Shape Leaders.* Boston Harvard Business School Press.

Benson, C., G. Palin, T. Cooney, and K. Farrell. (2012). "Agents of Change: Using Trans-formative Learning Theory to Enhance Social Entrepreneurship Education," http://sbaer.uca.edu/research/icsb/2012/Benson%20430.pdf (accessed July 22, 2013).

Burns, J. (2003). *Transforming Leadership: The Pursuit of Happiness.* Boston: Atlantic Monthly Press.

Caffarella, R. (2002). *Planning Programs for Adult Learners.* San Francisco: Jossey-Bass

Candy, P. (1991). *Self-Direction for Lifelong Learning: A Comprehensive Guide to Theory and Practice.* San Francisco: Jossey-Bass.

Cherry, K. (2013). "Experiential Learning: David Kolb's Theory of Learning," http://psychology.about.com/od/educationalpsychology/a/kolbs-learning-styles.htm (accessed July 22, 2013).

Clark, M. (1993). "Transformational Learning." *New Directions for Adult and Continuing Education,* 57:47-56.

Collins, M. (1994). *Adult Education as Vocation: A Critical Role for the Adult Educator,* 2nd edition. New York: Routledge.

Finch, A., and E. Rahim. (2011). "Adult Learning Styles and Technology-Driven Learning for Online Students." *Academic Leadership Journal,* 9(2): 21-28.

Gardner, H. (1993). *Multiple Intelligences: The Theory in Practice.* New York: Basic Books.

Gardner, H. (1999). *Multiple Intelligences for the 21st Century.* New York: Basic Books.

Gruber, H. (1973). "Piaget in the Classroom." In Schwebel, M., and J. Ralph (editors), *Courage and Cognitive Growth in Children and Scientists.* New York: Basic Books.

Heifetz, R., and M. Linsky. (2002). *Leadership on the Line: Staying Alive Through the Dangers of Leading.* Boston: Harvard Business School Press.

Heifetz, R., R. Sinder, A. Jones, L. Hodge, and K. Rowley. (1989). "Teaching and Assessing Leadership Courses at the John F. Kennedy School of Government." *Journal of Policy Analysis and Management*, 8(3): 536-562.

Imel, S. (1998). "Transformative Learning in Adulthood." Report No. EDO-CE-98-200. ERIC Document Reproduction Service No. ED423426. Columbus, OH: Adult, Career, and Vocational Education.

Johnstone, M., and M. Fern. (2010). "Case-in-Point: An Experiential Methodology for Leadership Education." *The Journal of Kansas Civic Leadership Development* 2(2): 98-117.

Johnstone, M., and M. Fern. (2008). "Intervention and Leadership: Tactical and Strategic Skills, can They Be Learned?" May 20. Unpublished manuscript, John F. Kennedy School of Executive Education, Harvard University, Cambridge, MA.

Kegan, R. (1982). *The Evolving Self: Problem and Process in Human Development.* Cambridge, MA: Harvard University Press.

Kegan, R., and L. Lahey. (2001). *How the Way We Talk Can Change the Way We Work.* San Francisco: Jossey-Bass.

Knowles, M. (1970). *The Modern Practice of Adult Education: Andragogy Versus Pedagogy.* Englewood Cliffs, NJ: Prentice Hall/Cambridge.

Kolb, D. (1984). *Experiential Learning: Experience as the Source of Learning and Development.* Englewood Cliffs, NJ: Prentice-Hall.

Kolb, D., R. Boyatzis, and C. Mainemelis. (2000). "Experiential Learning Theory: Previous Research and New Directions." In Sternberg, R., and L. Zhang (editors), *Perspectives on Cognitive, Learning, and Thinking Styles.* Hillsdale, NJ: Lawrence Erlbaum.

McCoy, M. (2006). "Teaching Style and the Application of Adult Learning Principles by Police Instructors." *Policing*, 29(1): 77.

Marsick, V., and K. Watkins. (2001). "Informal and Incidental Learning." *New Directions for Adult and Continuing Education*, 89:25-34.

Merriam, S. (Spring, 2001). "Andragogy and Self-Directed Learning: Pillars of Adult Learning Theory." In Merriam, S. (editor), *The New Update on Adult Learning Theory: New Directions for Adult and Continuing Education*, no. 89. San Francisco: Jossey-Bass.

Merriam, S., and R. Caffarella. (1999). *Learning in Adulthood,* 2nd edition. San Francisco: Jossey-Bass.

Mezirow, J. (1994). "Understanding Transformation Theory." *Adult Education Quarterly*, 44(4): 222-232.

Mezirow, J. (1997). "Transformative Learning: Theory to Practice." In Cranton, P. (editor), *New Directions for Adult and Continuing Education,* no. 74. San Francisco: Jossey-Bass.

Mezirow, J., and Associates, (editors). (2000). *Learning as Transformation: Critical Perspectives on a Theory in Progress.* San Francisco: Jossey-Bass.

Miettinen, R. (1998). "About the Legacy of Experiential Learning." *Lifelong Learning in Europe,* 4(3): 165-171.

National Guidelines for Educating EMS Instructors. (2002). "Facilitation Techniques," www.nhtsa.dot.gov/PEOPLE/injury/ems/Instructor/Module%2013%20-%20Facilitation%20Techniques.pdf#search='classroom%20facilitation (accessed July 22, 2013).

National Research and Development Centre for Adult Literacy and Numeracy. (2010). *Study on European Terminology in Adult Learning for a Common Language and Common Understanding and Monitoring of the Sector.* Commission Project EAC/11/2008. London: Institute of Education, University of London.

O'Neil, J., and S. Lamm. (2000). "Working as a Learning Coach Team in Action Learning." *New Directions for Adult and Continuing Education,* 87:43-52.

Parks, S.D. (2005). *Leadership Can be Taught: A Bold Approach for a Complex World,* 1st edition. Boston: Harvard Business Review Press.

Rager, K. (2003). "The Self-Directed Learning of Women With Breast Cancer." *Adult Education Quarterly,* 53(4): 277-293.

Raij, K. (2007). *Learning by Developing.* Laurea Publications A 58. Helsinki: Edita Prima Oy.

Record, K. (2004). "Facilitating: The Anti-Lecture," www.techlearning.com/features/0039/facilitation-the-anti-lecture/42254 (accessed July 22, 2013).

Ross, O. (2002). *Self-Directed learning in Adulthood: A Literature Review.* ERIC database ED 461050. Morehead, KY: Morehead State University.

Ruyle, J., and L. Geiselman. (1974). *Planning Non-Traditional Programs.* San Francisco: Jossey-Bass.

Steinbach, R. (2000) *Successful Lifelong Learning.* Menlo Park, CA: Crisp Learning.

Stewart, T. (2001). "Mystified by Training? Here are Some Clues." *Fortune,* 143:184.

Taylor, E. (1998). *The Theory And Practice Of Transformative Learning: A Critical Review.* Contract No. RR93002001. ERIC Document Reproduction Service No. ED423422. Columbus, OH: Center on Education and Training for Employment.

Wade, S., and M. Hammick. (1999). "Action Learning Circles: Action Learning in Theory and Practice." *Teaching in Higher Education,* 4:163-179.

Wynn, S. (2006). *Using Standards to Design Differentiated Learning Environments.* Boston: Pearson Custom Publishing.

Yi, J. (2005). "Effective Ways to Foster Learning." *Performance Improvement*, 44(1): 34-38.

Yorks, L., and E. Kasl. (May, 2002). "Toward a Theory and Practice for Whole-Person Learning: Reconceptualizing Experience and the Role of Affect." *Adult Education Quarterly*, 52(3): 176-192.

Chapter 2

What Makes a Classroom Facilitative?

This chapter will cover:

- building a facilitative learning environment
- classroom techniques and teaching styles
- managing participant resistance
- using your leadership to enable trainees' leadership.

THE VALUE OF THE RIGHT ENVIRONMENT

In the previous chapter we saw that adults very effectively learn leadership through the interactive, participant-driven, professionally relevant and cooperative approach known as facilitation. Our next task is to figure out how to build such a learning environment. Of course, proper theory and pointed techniques are absolutely necessary. But they're not enough. What really makes a classroom facilitative is the facilitator's and participants' reliable emotional presence in a relationship of trust.

Significantly, it's this same virtue of trustworthiness that makes genuine leadership—not just authority—possible. Facilitative leadership education instills in trainees the habits of listening, collaboration, speaking one's truth, and keeping one's principles by actually practicing and polishing these difficult, but essential, leadership qualities. Understanding the facilitative aims and techniques will let you strengthen exactly those traits in your leadership candidates.

VARIETIES AND ESSENCE OF FACILITATION: ACTIVE AND INTERACTIVE LEARNING

In chapter 1 you read that facilitation is the "lecture-replacement" teaching method that empowers participants by centering the learning environment around their experience and motivations. You also noted the spectrum of perspectives within the facilitative approach: One practitioner might hold that classrooms should be entirely democratic, while another directs fledgling groups; certain facilitators focus on group process, while others emphasize course content.

But despite these variances, all facilitators expect participants to apply their prior knowledge as they process new material together. That is, they agree that facilitative education means both active learning by participants as individuals, and interactive learning in groups, as well as interaction between them and the instructor. Especially as a leadership developer, you'll appreciate that energy and esprit de corps are fundamental executive qualities.

SPACE, TIME, AND TEACHING STYLES ENCOURAGE INTERACTIVE LEARNING

To help you strengthen those characteristics in your learners, we'll turn to basic methods that invite truly interactive learning.

Setting the Stage for Interactive Learning

To attain the active learning that facilitation demands, instructors need to create and maintain the most interactive environment possible. Current research tells us that compartmentalized, hierarchical, and rigid course structures actually discourage education. Child and Heavens (2003) reminded us that learning abilities are not only determined individually, but socially, since most teaching is offered by institutions; further, they found that institutions that very strictly separate fields or specializations within departments can hinder learning.

Conversely, then, facilitators can and should employ spatial, temporal, and stylistic arrangements that favor interactive learning. They can:

- Organize classroom space to remove physical barriers between themselves and participants, and among participants (such as podium-and-pews or assigned seats).
- Explicitly divvy up equal class time for each member's comments and for group and subgroup discussions.
- Present essential information verbally, visually, and experientially.

Good facilitators shape the teaching environment itself not just to permit, but to pursue, the creative interplay of persons, opinions, and learning preferences.

Having set the physical stage for learner-driven education even before the first session (for details, see Part III, chapter 7), facilitators can direct less during class and allow learners to mold the material to their interests, trusting them to negotiate classroom decisions. So right away facilitators encourage discussion, role-playing, group research, and presentations—tasks Indiana University physics professor Richard Hake (1998) recognizes as "designed . . . to promote conceptual understanding through interactive engagement of students in heads-on (always) and hands-on (usually) activities which yield immediate feedback through discussion with peers and/or instructors." Quick, constant confirming or correcting benefits your trainees doubly: It models how to balance leadership qualities of openness and decisiveness, because you are listening and responding to them as individuals and, at the same time, you are focusing on the course agenda.

Facilitators expect that they and class members will jointly set course objectives and assessment criteria and strive for equal participation from all learners, however differently abled. To fulfill these intentions, Anderson (2007), Record (2004), and many others caution that instructors must offer what educators call differentiated instruction—built-in options in what material course takers will learn, how they will learn, and how their learning will be evaluated.

Why Leadership Facilitators Use Differentiated Instruction

The justification for using differentiated instruction in teaching both children and adults draws upon the insight of the early-twentieth-century Russian psychologist Lev Vygotsky, who said that individuals learn best when the information taught is appropriate to their ability to function in society. According to educational psychologist Kathie Nunley (2006), differentiated instruction has become an essential part of all American educators' repertoire over the past 40 years as the cultural make-up of American classrooms has become increasingly heterogeneous.

While most "constructivist" (social preparedness) learning theorists focus on children, we saw that facilitation accepts and welcomes different learning styles among adults and holds that, for mature persons as well, course content and delivery should match their intellectual and social readiness to grasp it. Contemporary instructors enrich this social preparedness view through cutting-edge research into the neuropsychological development of the brain and personality (Anderson 2007). And we already know that facilitative theory accepts and encourages the life-long evolution and expansion of adults' learning modes. In fact, facilitative leadership development in particular expects transformative evolution of trainees and trainer alike by requiring openness to new ideas, polishing skill in mirroring others' expressions, and integrating widely different viewpoints and talents into collectively envisioned and achieved goals.

How Facilitators Use Differentiated Instruction

Differentiated instruction directs the educator to deploy a variety of teaching methods to suit students' varied learning profiles. For example, they may blend whole-class, group, and individual instruction; use varied verbal, non-verbal, auditory, visual, and kinesthetic (moving) approaches to convey core information; and apply differing modes of artistic, performance, individual, and collective evaluation. As Tomlinson and Allan (2000) put it, the learner-centered model asks instructors to tailor instruction to learners, rather than requiring learners to bend themselves to the curriculum. Participants' social, intellectual, and emotional maturity, interests, and abilities directly shape course content, presentation, and testing.

Equally important, the transformation of trainees' interactive and reflective qualities through facilitative education encourages teachers and participants to constantly reshape course curriculum, approach, and evaluation. (For plenty of ideas on how to deliver differentiated instruction in your leadership course, see Part III, chapter 6 and chapter 7.) With practice, you'll come to offer multiple slants on what you're conveying without absorbing too much class time.

Case in Point: Differentiation, Not Self-Immolation

In one class, I tried six ways to Sunday to tailor my instruction to reach a few participants with poor educational backgrounds. But rather than being respected as creative and inclusive, I was resented as disorganized and dumbing-down. I learned that "differentiated education" means varying my style and offering alternative assignments, but not doing gymnastics for a few on class time.

Facilitator Skills

Because the success of facilitation hinges on active participation, it demands different skills than lecturing. As noted earlier, facilitators fulfill the same tasks as do conventional instructors, but they must accomplish them by motivating class member contributions:

- They introduce new material, but do so by steering class members to information sources rather than giving them "the answer."
- They assess learning, but negotiate grading criteria with participants.
- They clarify the course purpose, but survey learners' interests to set agendas and formats collectively.
- They field questions, but reroute authority to the group as researchers rather than as passive note-takers.

So while the instructor proposes ideas and moves the course along, at every step he or she needs participants' input and consent.

Enabling trainees to attain their agreed-upon aims means that often, instructors must spark discussion, summarize information and reactions, and mediate disputes. Hootstein (2002) defines the facilitator as an informed expert and resource provider, director of agenda, creator of collaborative environments, and model of proficiency. Berge (1995) and Liu (2005) view the facilitator's roles as pedagogical (creating a learning environment and contributing specialized knowledge), managerial (organizational, procedural, and administrative), and technical (acclimating students to the system). Additional functions include setting the pace and assessing performance, as well as establishing the intellectual and social environment for learning. In brief, surveying the major writers on the topic tells us that the facilitator works as a consultant, gadfly, cheering section, and referee as needed to widen participation, refocus discussion, rein in the talkative, and curtail emotional outbursts.

Fundamental to all these roles, and to your central aim of eliciting general participation, is the ability to mirror—accurately summarize and express—participants' comments. Without your concise re-presentation of possibly unclear statements, participants who cannot make themselves understood (or who do not feel understood) tend either to repeat themselves with escalating volume or withdraw. Providing a verbal synopsis of remarks, relating one member's ideas to another's, inviting expansion or completion of a cut-off sentence—these are some of the most effective ways facilitators can keep participation both universal and productive.

Case in Point: Say It Back

One class member's presentation went poorly, and furrowed brows and exasperated looks showed that no one understood what he had meant to say. In frustration, he lashed out furiously at a classmate for giving him "bad advice" on his project, nearly reducing her to tears. I had to weigh how much of the incident I should process without turning the class into a group therapy session. I elected to state in front of the class, briefly, that the presenter did not feel he had expressed himself well, and blamed a classmate. I then walked over to the targeted person and asked her if she was alright. At that point the offending participant stood up and apologized both to the class and the targeted classmate.

In other words, skilled facilitators must grasp and respectfully acknowledge group members' feelings as well as ideas. For interactive learning to occur—or even to be tolerated—strong emotions arising from disputes or airing deeply held beliefs must be recognized and directed positively, or class communication may be permanently damaged. Facilitators must have problem-solving options at the ready to overcome any impasse: reframing the issue, dividing participants into small brainstorming groups, calling for a short break, or noting where disputants actually agree. Another way they recognize members' concerns is taking advantage of "teachable moments"—unplanned opportunities that arise spontaneously in class but provide the perfect instance for presenting important information or ideas. Great facilitators rejoice in these fleeting opportunities because they reveal students' genuine interests, and often let them blossom into a full-blown lesson.

Case in Point: Correction Delayed is Correction Denied

Despite a collective outlawing of side conversations, texting, and phoning, these behaviors became rampant in one of my classes. Repeatedly throughout the course, I asked trainees to review our code of conduct, but to little avail. On the last night of class, a crucial group presentation was interrupted continually by a couple of class members texting and chatting. I pointed out that the presenters were permitting the very actions they had prohibited at the beginning. To my surprise, instead of appreciating and applying my intervention, the group—including the presenters!—became upset with my "changing the rules on them."

I was forewarned and ready the next time. In another class, a perennial late-comer loudly announced his entry, let his phone jangle, answered it at the top of his voice, and announced to titters that "it was just a telemarketer." Worse, no one complained. I was disappointed in the collective passivity about breaking group rules. But I knew to channel my feelings into a leadership lesson rather than indulge them in admonishment or regulations.

I began the next session with a new icebreaker. Dividing the class into four groups, I asked each to list the work behaviors they most valued. From this list, each group would compose guidelines for professional conduct, write them on the board, and justify them to the class. The resulting four guidelines were stunningly identical, specifying tardiness, rudeness, and divided focus as inadmissible. Only then did I let myself point out that they were regularly tolerating violations of precisely these basic expectations in class. Then, the whole group formally wrote up the regulations they agreed to maintain throughout the program. At the close of that session I explained that I had not exerted my authority to end the chaos earlier, preferring the deeper experiential learning they would take outside the classroom.

After this, all side conversations, phone use, and tardiness stopped cold. On the course evaluation one respondent noted that the experience "exemplified what leadership is, tied this whole program together, and brought leadership into our being. It made visible the need for leaders to look inward so we can demonstrate that to others. The dynamics of the class took an obvious turn for the better . . .. As [President] Lincoln states: 'If you are a good leader, when your work is done, your aim fulfilled, your people will say, 'We did this ourselves.'"

But while they may need to smooth group workings, facilitators remain neutral about the actual outcome of discussions and let the team lead. Boyd and Myers (1988), and King (2005), direct educators to practice, first, seasoned guidance—the ability to serve as an experienced mentor who can help others transform themselves—and, second, compassionate criticism that helps students question and work out their own world view.

It follows that there are specific behaviors instructors should avoid:

- praising, or criticizing, ideas of individual participants
- pushing their own ideas

- making new class rules without consulting participants
- making lengthy comments.

The National Guidelines for Educating EMS Instructors tell us that to help your participants operate as independent active learners, you need, above all, to understand group members as people. In addition, you must demonstrate planning, communication, growth, problem identification, and problem-solving behaviors—in short, the same behaviors you hope to strengthen in trainees.

When you ask people to think back on those who inspired them most, they very often name a teacher (and often, an early one). But they almost never ascribe the impact to that teacher's subject matter. They rarely cite geometry or Spanish as a guiding force in their lives. What they'll tell you is that the teacher "believed in me when nobody else did," "taught me to try again after messing up," "pushed me to develop my gift," or "worked me hard but was always there to help."

Although we don't usually consider schoolteachers as executives, it's clear that those who value individual students enough to demand their very best do, in fact, function brilliantly as genuine leaders. And as a leadership developer, you get the chance to inspire your trainees in exactly the same way. You do not teach leadership as a subject matter, but by modeling leader-like qualities and expecting them in your trainees: appreciation of others, encouragement of individual talents, holding to standards, and personal trustworthiness.

THE BIG PROBLEM: PARTICIPANT RESISTANCE TO ACTIVE LEARNING

Unfortunately, your virtues alone won't suffice in facilitative instruction, where participants bear at least as much responsibility for their learning as the teacher. That they don't always accept this duty is graphically illustrated by a student comment Benvenuto (1999) cites: "Get up to the f---ing board—that's what we pay you for!" One reason for such reactions is that, for many, active learning in a group is hard, even painful. Facilitation questions the long-standing perception that "good students" are obedient, passive learners, and insists that they become entrepreneurial, strategic learners. This new view implies new rules, namely that learners should:

- try to transcend past attitudes about learning
- question ideas absorbed from other persons or institutions
- view their life experience as making them more, not less, open to change
- consider different beliefs with respect
- use both rational and emotional mental processes
- integrate critical reflection into their class work and personal life.

If class members seem asleep and I think I'm seeing simple boredom, I've learned to employ what I hope is humor and what I know is tact to comment on the body language I observe, and suggest the class discuss its meaning. Perhaps shocked by the honesty, listeners generally straighten up and pay attention, air their gripes, listen to their classmates, and reapply themselves to work. I ask particularly resistant group members to meet with me outside class, also usually to good effect. And as every Scoutmaster knows, putting problem kids "in charge" can turn them around by making them invested in the group's success; most often I get similar results by pointedly inviting disgruntled learners to help plan upcoming units. For truly stubborn cases, I first consult my colleagues for a fresh perspective, but I am ready to drop an enrollee if need be, and I make sure tough customers know it.

THE BIG SECRET: INTERACTIVE LEARNING REQUIRES RELATIONSHIPS

So facilitation won't work just by moving seats around, matching material and delivery to folks' interests and skills, and accurately summarizing their comments. To function, it has to restructure the traditional student-teacher interaction to favor learners' active acquisition of information that may shake older certainties and introduce new notions. Thus, while active learning may be the most effective means of educating adults, it is by no means the easiest. It requires a participant-facilitator relationship of respect and trust to allow the expression of opposing views, newly noticed doubts, and genuine growth.

Case in Point: Support Your Local Bully

I had a bona fide bully in one class who counted on others' following the path of least resistance rather than speaking up. In one incident he insisted on doing a group project he had already done for three other courses. When I reminded him the project had to be a new, cooperative creation, he visibly sulked and actually grew more upset as his group relaxed and listened to previously silent group members.

I wasn't surprised when he came to my office to ask how to drop the class. But I didn't answer his ostensible question. I simply said that this class was presenting him with some very new experiences, but I was confident he could handle them fine. He left without a word. And not only did he stay in the class, in ensuing sessions he became increasingly relieved and interested.

According to Creighton (2005), whenever people work together they are communicating on at least two levels: the level of factual content and the level of their relationship. In the traditional lecture-based classroom, "factual" communication receives all the attention, while "relationship" communication is only rarely mentioned. Nonetheless, the relationship is constantly conveyed by every single classroom event: who gets to speak and for how long, whose needs take precedence, or who gets cut off or put down. In other words, each detail of how the class is run—its "process"—constantly transmits each participant's relationship to colleagues and to the instructor.

The learner-centered education model that's so prevalent in adult education theory actually originated in educational psychology. So it's not surprising that theorists in this field, such as Cornelius-White (2007), noticed that optimal learning occurs only in the context of an honest and consistent interpersonal connection between learner and instructor. Because facilitation combines the characteristics of experiential, self-directed, transformational, and group approaches, the relationships between facilitator and participants, and among groups and subgroups of participants, form the foundation of all classroom learning.

Modeling Qualities

Clearly, by modeling good teaching, facilitators prepare participants to lead group learning activities themselves. Cranton (2006) makes a subtler point: The good teacher is actually modeling the "good student" who is willing to learn and to change. Taylor (1998) and King (2005) point out that a teacher's mature quality of critical reflection helps students connect the sometimes conflicting rational and emotional aspects of the facilitative classroom experience. So, the facilitator's first job is to create a climate of safety and sensitivity. Heifetz, Grashow, and Linsky (2009) specified that such an environment lets participants question their own and others' preconceptions and try out new solutions together. Especially in programs that seek to develop executive strengths, you as a facilitator need to do exactly what you expect from trainees: try to transcend personal beliefs and understand different ones; cultivate and celebrate alternate ways of learning; establish trust, encourage caring, and reflect on one's own experience in order to help others.

Borrowing from the work of Heifetz and Linsky (2002), Parks (2005) notes that gifted facilitators demonstrate genuine leadership for their trainees: They stay "on the balcony" rather than direct—or, worse, star in—the show; they "orchestrate the conflict" by using classroom stress to reveal competing values; they "give the work back" to participants; and they always "hold steady" under fire. To ensure completion of the agenda they identify and address counterproductive group dynamics by drawing out the introverted, protecting the targeted, redirecting meanderers, and restraining the aggressive. Similarly they attend to the group process as a whole in order to encourage free and vibrant, but fair and constructive, debate and decision-making.

In fact, your sensitivity to and resolution of subtle frictions in this microcosmic society expresses the same leadership traits participants will internalize. Above all, as an able facilitator you'll model the emotional, intellectual, moral, and mental qualities of character crucial to leading—chiefly integrity, initiative, and respect for self and others. Having integrity means conducting oneself according to ethical standards. In the classroom, this means you as the facilitator do what you promise, explain your motives honestly, and treat all participants equally. By initiative, we mean that you as the facilitator can start and support an interactive, constructive, and effective group process. In your facilitative role you show respect for self and others by expecting, and valuing, all group members' efforts, and by acting as a just referee in disputes.

Ethical Duties of Facilitators

It might be reasonably argued that all good instructors possess the virtues of integrity, initiative, and respect for self and others. But because facilitative learning has such power to transform participants' views and stir troubling emotions, it poses particular ethical challenges and so requires especially careful behavior from the instructors. For example, Boyd and Myers (1998) and King (2005) consider grieving as a necessary and critical phase in transformational learning, as learners must be allowed to mourn the loss of old patterns of thinking before they can adopt new ones. Daloz (1999) concurs that growth can be frightening as learners have to let go of old concepts of self and the world. Comparing transformation to a journey in which the mentor serves as gatekeeper and guide, he reminds instructors to structure their courses to maximize learners' profound personal development rather than their merely technical competence.

Many other emotional hazards in the facilitative classroom demand equal sensitivity: transference and counter-transference (learners' and instructors' unconscious emotional investments in each other); keeping confidentiality within and outside the classroom; managing the shock of cognitive dissonance; and discussions of "hot button" topics too intense for some to handle. And because facilitation aims squarely to transform ideas and behaviors, even your subtlest disapproval can destroy participants' sense of safety and, in turn, their ability to take in and apply new concepts. Starbuck and Hedberg (2003) remind us that positive outcomes are much more likely to result in successful learning than are negative ones. Their research supports the idea that facilitation, like all transformational teaching, rests on trust. Good instructors know that recognizing success helps people learn; great facilitators know that giving participants the "license to fail" without fear of humiliation is key to their personal as well as professional growth.

Given the personal challenges and changes facilitative education invites, Baumgartner (2001) confronts perhaps its deepest moral question: whether instructors even have a right to practice transformational learning. Reminding instructors that transformational learning frequently brings up disturbing emotions for both learners and teachers, she emphasizes the need to build a caring relationship between all parties. She also recommends that the instructor and learners design a formal code of classroom ethics together, and further encourages instructors to support each other in a learning forum. Thus (although with minimal interference) facilitators must:

- Supervise the writing of a classroom code of ethics.
- Suggest options to help the class or small groups overcome impasses.
- Defuse personal conflicts between students.
- Avoid discussing exceptionally disruptive topics or beliefs.
- Assess and calm strong emotional reactions in learners.
- Keep the discussion tone educational rather than therapeutic.

Case in Point: You're the Leader

I once had a course enrollee who adamantly insisted that we needed to conduct 360-degree feedbacks (universal performance reviews) in class. I had a gut feeling it wasn't appropriate for the group at that stage, so turned down his request without negotiation. I then worried for days that I had been authoritarian. But the more stridently he repeated his demand, the more clearly I could put my finger on the reason for my instinctive veto: I had unconsciously realized that his real motive was a passive-aggressive wish to critique others. From this I learned to honor my own judgment in protecting the psychological safety of the class.

SUMMARY

The ethical foundation of facilitation supports both teaching and learning leadership. If we need further proof that facilitation works because of the trusting relationship built between participants and the instructor, let's consider the special demands it places on the facilitator. Although all interactive approaches fire up participants' feelings, facilitation requires that the instructor moderate group dynamics fairly to let group members freely compose, and then faithfully follow, class rules and agenda. Further, an able facilitator must create a relaxed, reliable, and psychologically safe ambiance for collaborative problem-solving and for the transformative experiences of the facilitative classroom. Most important, class members learn by observing the instructor manage issues and procedures. That is, your trainees can practice leadership only if they experience your integrity, initiative, and respect for self and others. Then their work in groups and as class leaders increases their appreciation not only of your knowledge, but of your character.

So the fundamental role of trust in facilitation is not just an ideal. It is a fact that effective leadership really means ethical leadership. Heading a business or public organization without respecting others enough to learn from them and to maintain their trust limits leadership as well as loyalty. If you understand this truth, you understand why facilitation is the optimal leadership training approach for both teachers and trainees. In the next chapter, through the lens of group dynamics theory, we'll see exactly how the ethical concerns of facilitative leadership training transform learners into leaders.

REFLECTION AND NEXT STEPS

1. **Consider your comfort.** In what ways does contemplating facilitative teaching make you uneasy? What techniques or aims do you use already that resemble facilitation? How might recalling your own student days—the best and the worst—inspire you to teach in a facilitative, interactive, and cooperative way?

2. **Every classroom presents a mix**. Can you see yourself using differentiated instruction—a variety of presentation styles to suit different participants' strengths—or does this feel like "dummying down" to you? How might you make knowledge accessible to different types of learners?

3. **Find opportunities out of class to practice the art of mirroring**. How does it change your listening when you know you've got to mirror someone else's ideas and feelings back? What's the hardest

part of mirroring for you? What might help you understand and communicate others' messages better?

REFERENCES AND RESOURCES

Anderson, K. (2007). "Differentiated Instruction to Include All Students." *Preventing School Failure*, 51(3): 49-54.

Baumgartner, L. (2001). "An Update on Transformational Learning Theory." In Merriam, S. (editor), *The New Update on Adult Learning Theory: New Directions for Adult and Continuing Education*. San Francisco: Jossey-Bass.

Baxter Magolda, M. (January-February, 2012). "Building Learning Partnerships." *Change: The Magazine of Higher Learning*, www.changemag.org/Archives/Back%20 Issues/2012/January-February%202012/learning-partnerships-full.html (accessed July 22, 2013).

Benvenuto, M. (June, 1999). "In an Age of Interactive Learning, Some Students Want the Same Old Song and Dance." *Chronicle of Higher Education*, 45(39): B9.

Berge, Z. (1995). "Facilitating Computer Conferencing: Recommendations From the Field." *Educational Technology*, 35(1): 22-30.

Boyd, R., and J. Myers. (1988). "Transformative Education." *International Journal of Lifelong Education*, 7(4): 261-284.

Child, J., and S. Heavens. (2003). "The Social Constitution of Organizations and its Implications for Organizational Learning." In Dierkes, M., A. Berthoin Antal, J. Child, and I. Nonaka (editors), *Handbook of Organizational Learning and Knowledge*. New York: Oxford University Press.

Comings, J., B. Garner, and C. Smith (editors). (2003). *The Review of Adult Learning and Literacy*, 4. Mahway, NJ: Lawrence Erlbaum.

Conlan, J., S. Grabowski, and K. Smith. (2003). "Adult Learning." In *Emerging Perspectives on Learning, Teaching, and Technology*, Orey, M. (editor) http://projects.coe.uga.edu/epltt/ (accessed July 22, 2013).

Cornelius-White, J. (2007). "Learner-Centered Teacher-Student Relationships Are Effective: A Meta-Analysis." *Review of Educational Research*, 77(1): 113-143.

Cranton, P. (2006). *Understanding and Promoting Transformative Learning: A Guide for Educators of Adults*, 2nd edition. San Francisco: Jossey-Bass.

Creighton, T. (2005). *Leading From Below the Surface: A Non-Traditional Approach to School Leadership*. Thousand Oaks, CA: Corwin Press.

Daloz, L. (1999). *Mentor: Guiding the Journey of Adult Learners*. San Francisco: Jossey-Bass.

Eller, J. (2004). *Effective Group Facilitation in Education: How to Energize Meetings and Manage Difficult Groups*. Thousand Oaks, CA: Corwin Press.

Ellis, E., R. Gable, M. Gregg, and M. Rock. (2008). "REACH: A Framework for Differentiating Classroom Instruction." *Preventing School Failure*, 52(2): 31-47.

Feenberg, A., and C. Xin. (February, 2010). "What Is Facilitation?," http://base.dp-h.info/es/fiches/dph/fiche-dph-8213.html (accessed July 22, 2013).

Hake, R. (1998). "Interactive-Engagement Versus Traditional Methods: A Six-Thousand-Student Survey of Mechanics Test Data for Introductory Physics Courses." *American Journal of Physics*, 66(1): 64-74, http://dx.doi.org/10.1119/1.18809 (accessed July 22, 2013).

Heath, C., and D. Heath. (2010). *Switch: How to Change Things When Change is Hard*. New York: Crown Publishing.

Heifetz, R., A. Grashow, and M. Linsky. (2009). *The Practice of Adaptive Leadership: Tools and Tactics for Changing Your Organization and the World*. Boston: Harvard Business Review Press.

Heifetz, R., and M. Linsky. (2002). *Leadership on the Line: Staying Alive Through the Dangers of Leading*. Boston: Harvard Business School Press.

Hootstein, E. (2002). "Wearing Four Pairs of Shoes: The Roles of E-Learning Facilitators." *Association for the Advancement of Computing in Education* (AACE), www.astd.org/LC/2002/1002_hootstein.htm (accessed July 22, 2013).

Jenkins, D. (2012). "Exploring Signature Pedagogies in Undergraduate Leadership Education." *Journal of Leadership Education*, 11(1): 1-27.

Kegan, R., and L. Lahey. (2009). *Immunity to Change: How to Overcome It and Unlock Potential in Yourself and Your Organization*. Boston: Harvard Business Review Press.

King, K. (2005). *Bringing Transformative Learning to Life*. Malabar, FL: Krieger.

Levy, H. (2008). "Meeting the Needs of All Students Through Differentiated Instruction: Helping Every Child Reach and Exceed Standards." *The Clearing House*, 81(4): 161-164.

Liu, X., C. Bonk, R. Magjuka, S. Lee, and B. Su. (2005). "Exploring Four Dimensions of Online Instructor Roles: A Program Level Case Study." *Journal of Asynchronous Learning Networks*, 9(4): 29-48.

National Guidelines for Educating EMS Instructors. (2002). "Facilitation Techniques," www.nhtsa.dot.gov/PEOPLE/injury/ems/Instructor/Module%2013%20-%20Facilitation%20Techniques.pdf#search='classroom%20facilitation (accessed July 22, 2013).

Nunley, K. (2006). *Differentiating the High School Classroom: Solution Strategies for 18 Common Obstacles.* Thousand Oaks, CA: Corwin Press.

Parks, S.D. (2005). *Leadership Can Be Taught: A Bold Approach for a Complex World*, 1st edition. Boston: Harvard Business Review Press.

Rebora, A. (2008). "Making a Difference." *Teacher Magazine*, 2(1): 26, 28-31.

Record, K. (2004). "Facilitating: The Anti-Lecture," http://www.techlearning.com/features/0039/facilitation-the-anti-lecture/42254 (accessed July 22, 2013).

Shea, P., C.S. Li, K. Swan, and A. Pickett.(2005). "Developing Learning Community in Online Asynchronous College Courses: The Role of Teaching Presence." *Journal of Asynchronous Learning Networks*, 9(4): 59-82.

Starbuck, W., and B. Hedberg. (2003). "How Organizations Learn from Success and Failure." In Dierkes, M., A. Berthoin Antal, J. Child, and I. Nonaka (editors), *Handbook of Organizational Learning and Knowledge,* New York: Oxford University Press.

Taylor, E. (1998). *The Theory and Practice of Transformative Learning: A Critical Review.* Contract No. RR93002001. ERIC Document Reproduction Service No. ED423422. Columbus, OH: Center on Education and Training for Employment.

Tomlinson, C. (2001). *How to Differentiate Instruction in Mixed-Ability Classrooms*, 2nd edition. Alexandria, VA: ASCD.

Tomlinson, C., and S. Allan. (2000). *Leadership for Differentiating Schools and Classrooms.* Alexandria, VA: ASCD.

Vlachopoulos, P., and J. Cowan. (November, 2010). "Choices of Approaches in E-Moderation: Conclusions From a Grounded Theory Study." *Active Learning in Higher Education*, 11(3): 213-224, doi:10.1177/1469787410379684.

Chapter 3

Group Dynamics and Facilitative Training

This chapter will cover:

- explanation of group dynamics theory and basic terms
- how groups form and evolve
- how group types and member roles vary
- identifying difficult behaviors
- testing group dynamics theory right in the facilitative classroom
- tracking group dynamics in your class
- using your class as a laboratory for learning leadership and a gym for exercising it
- the real—not just ideal—link between ethics and effective leadership.

GROUP DYNAMICS THEORY

The modern study of group dynamics spontaneously emerged in many countries in the late 1940s, soon after the end of World War II. The horrors of that war intensified concerns about abusive leadership; groups of average people behaving with unbelievable cruelty to other groups; and national groups accepting their country's destructive, and self-destructive, policies. Group dynamics theory sought to describe and explain these and other collective behaviors.

As a leadership educator, understanding and teaching group dynamics is crucial because, clearly, leaders are only leaders if they have people to guide. And that collectivity consists of smaller subgroups (say, workers and managers, or officers of different ranks) who deal with other groups (such as suppliers, inspectors, advertisers, customers, competitors, or communities). Leaders need to grasp not only their relations with those groups, but the internal functioning within, and the interactions among, those collectivities themselves. As a facilitative trainer in leadership, you enjoy the stunning advantage of letting participants not only study, but experience, the fascinating processes by which groups form, function, and sometimes fizzle. You want your trainees to feel, like one graduate of a facilitative leadership program, that they "learned to collaborate and display leadership while working in groups by exchanging ideas in a positive and supportive environment."

Definitions of Group and Group Dynamics

While terms vary, group dynamics theories almost uniformly define a *group* as two or more individuals related in some way, and *group dynamics* as the characteristic attitudes and behaviors impacting a group's formation, structure, and workings. These evolving relational patterns within groups noted by Beck and Lewis (2002) and Yalom and Leszcz (2005) may be either observable or inferred: Beck and Lewis define "observable processes" as verbal or nonverbal communication, while "inferred" or "covert group processes" include conscious and unconscious intentions, motivations, and needs of separate individuals, dyads (pairs), subgroups, or the group as a whole. Hartman and Gibbard (1974), Schein (2004), and Smith (2005) concur that both observable and inferred processes may serve "adaptive," work-oriented ends or "defensive," work-avoidant purposes.

Although agreeing on those basic definitions, group dynamics theories diverge when considering why and how groups develop. Among main schools of thought, Homans's (1974) social exchange theory, based on behavioral psychology, argues that groups evolve through activities, interactions, and sentiments: As individuals share activities, they interact and develop attitudes (positive or negative) toward each other. Other social exchange theories explain group establishment as a result of an individual's expectation of mutual advantages based on trust and shared obligation. In other words, people form an affiliation if they think relationships within a collectivity will benefit them all. In contrast, social identity theory suggests that individuals join and contribute to a demographically, culturally, or organizationally identifiable group because membership in it gives them a sense of belonging and self-worth.

In addition to explaining why groups form, group dynamics theory examines how they develop. Focusing on the stages of group maturation implies that groups rarely perform at their best from the start, but must successfully negotiate predictable phases to become productive—a valuable insight for facilitative leadership developers! According to Tuckman (1965), all groups move through the five phases of birth, power struggles, rule-setting, work, and completion—steps he conveniently names forming, storming, norming, performing, and adjourning. Each step brings up specific issues that group members must successfully manage in order to maintain group efficacy and to advance to the next stage. And each stage demonstrates typical structures and potential snags in the basic operations of communication, participation, decision-making, and roles.

Structural Classification of Groups and Member Roles

We can categorize groups either by their structure (organization) or their function (behavior). (See Part III for a great activity, Paging Dr. Freud, to help you teach the basics of group structure and function.) Although in healthy groups the structure meshes beautifully with the function, we can look separately at these two angles, just as medical students might study human anatomy separately from human physiology. We'll start with the structural way to describe groups as it's easier to see. The most fundamental way to classify a group structurally is to ask whether it's formal or informal. Formal groups are established by an organization to achieve its goals, while informal groups—even within an organization—spring naturally from group members' common interests and may focus on fun or self-improvement as well as on a task.

Formal Group Types: Command, Task, and Functional

Institutions may form command groups, usually consisting of a supervisor and subordinates, for ongoing and varying work. Academic departments with a chairperson, faculty, and staff; crisis teams in emergency services; and the military all qualify as command groups. Organizations may also establish (and disband) more limited task groups (or task forces) with appointed members and jobs. This category includes project groups, committees—either ad hoc (temporary) or standing (permanent, usually with rotating membership)—and any group given a discrete mission within a specified time period. Their aims may be developing a new product, organizing the employee picnic, or improving production. Organizations may also create functional groups to accomplish particular goals without any specific time frame—for example, departments for marketing, customer service, or accounting.

Informal Group Types: Interest or Friendship

In contrast to formal groups, informal groups coalesce and recruit pretty spontaneously in response to individuals' shared interests or values. They include hobby clubs, social circles, literary or political salons, business networks, or lunch, exercise, or sports groups. Generally, they congregate without any larger organizational purpose and without any time frame. But informal groups can exert a strong influence—positive or negative—within organizations: Employees may assemble to devise an improved production process, or to share shortcuts that jeopardize quality.

Interest groups usually survive longer than less focused ones. Their members may belong to different organizations or departments but are bound together by some common concern, like students in a study group, employees desiring greener company policies, or aspiring Toastmasters. Folks in more general friendship groups may in fact share causes or religious persuasions, but primarily value each other's company. Company employees in a friendship group may exercise together, play softball on weekends, or host monthly potluck lunches.

Group Size

In addition to formality or informality, aspects of group structure like size, member roles, rules, and cohesiveness help us categorize them. We noted that groups can number from two upwards, but as they grow we see what's called the Ringelmann effect (after the French agricultural engineer who described it in 1913): As group size increases, member satisfaction increases—but only up to a point! For example, Levinger (2010) suggests, a group of six allows twice as many interactions as does a group of three, but expanding it beyond about 12 lowers satisfaction since members feel less cohesion. So groups of seven to 12 seem optimal for encouraging universal participation but avoiding angst over turn-taking. These insights help you as a facilitator of group learning to determine whether a given activity works better with small subgroups, larger subgroups, or the entire class.

Group Member Roles: Task, Maintenance, and Blocking

In formal groups, member roles with specific duties (like president, vice president, treasurer, or secretary) have usually been predetermined. But like all groups, even formal ones engender informal (and sometimes unacknowledged) member roles such as social smoothers, hard workers, or experts in a given area. In addition, new roles may spring up naturally to meet a group's emerging needs. Those new roles may even replace assigned ones as group members become clearer about their task and more assertive about how to accomplish it. Finally, individuals may elect themselves to fulfill particular roles—but rarely for common ends or with universal approval. Formally assigned or not, group roles fall into rough categories: useful task roles and maintenance roles, and harmful blocking roles.

Task roles—including initiator-contributor, information seeker and supplier, clarifier, energizer, summarizer, recorder, and reality-tester—relate directly to accomplishing an accepted group goal. The initiator defines a task, proposes actions, and suggests procedures; information seekers and suppliers find and present facts; clarifiers interpret ideas, define terms, and explain issues; summarizers analyze and restate arguments; and reality-testers point out on-the-ground problems.

Maintenance roles emerge informally to smooth relationships and functions among group members. These social-emotional activists include the harmonizer, gatekeeper, consensus-tester, encourager, and compromiser. The harmonizer seeks to reduce group tension and reconcile differences. Gatekeepers maintain universal communication channels. The consensus-tester helps the group come to a decision. Encouragers engage members through warm camaraderie and responsiveness, and the compromiser modifies decisions, brokers deals, and admits errors to grease the group process.

In contrast, blocking roles, while also found nearly universally, are wholly free of collective purpose and, in fact, usually frustrate it. The self-centered roles of the aggressor, dominator, attention-seeker, or distracter aim—even if unconsciously—to satisfy only personal needs, and actually disrupt the group. They do this by monopolizing discussion, verbally attacking other group members, or distracting them with trivia or an unceasing stream of jokes. Often the blocking behavior may not be intended as negative; a member may habitually spew wisecracks to break his or her own tension, may honestly regret a decision agreed to earlier, or may have an unconscious pattern of avoiding work. But conscious or not, blocking roles can destroy individuals' sense of safety and the group's cohesion, efficacy, energy, and joy.

Aggressors in particular threaten group function by criticizing members' values, often with sarcastic or passive-aggressive humor, thus expressing a hostility of character that lies far deeper than any classroom situation could reasonably elicit. Dominators attempt to control conversations and dictate group decisions by interrupting others and endlessly asserting their own authority. Attention-seekers can't stand equal opportunities for all to share the limelight—exactly what you are trying to ensure—and pull the focus back on them through any means. Distracters, who often play the charming comedian, have abandoned the group psychologically even though they remain in it physically, and seek so many "breaks" in the work that it stymies group objectives. All these blocking or avoidance behaviors, by definition, help people evade genuine interaction, because all blockers follow a hidden (and usually unconscious) agenda divorced from the group. As a facilitative leadership instructor, you'll soon come to distinguish arguments fueled by personality from those inspired by philosophy. More important, you'll model for your trainees how the genuine leader can manage and utilize both.

I have had my share of difficult group members. I'm sure each of us has our pet problem child, but for me, learners who demonstrate arrogance or entitlement, or who subvert group aims, are all equally trying. Arrogant participants thought they knew more than me or their classmates because they read "all the books," but had no idea how to apply the material and, what was worse, didn't see—or care—how they affected class members on whom they imposed their ideas. Entitled over-achievers, when criticized even with respect and diplomacy, blindly lashed out in accusations and blame. Self-proclaimed leaders usually had no one actually following them, but frightened others from contributing. Participants who, sometimes with considerable wit, distracted or hijacked the group into off-topic activities, disrupted the flow of the class, and crippled the power of the group to manage its own learning. I guess that all these difficult cases share the same flaw: Actively or passively, they all wanted to dictate instead of lead. That desire augured poorly for developing their leadership qualities and forced me to work doubly hard: first to rein them in so others could learn, and then to wrest them from their habitual blocking roles, so they could learn.

Role Ambiguity and Role Conflict

Any discrepancy between a learner's set role and the way he or she understands it creates ambiguity. In formal groups especially, supervisors assign roles. But vague descriptions of delegated responsibilities just confuse people. Such ambiguity in supervisors' directives stokes group members' dissatisfaction and can provoke their (physical or psychological) departure from the collective.

In addition to unclearness, inconsistency between an assigned role and the way it's performed creates two types of role conflict. Inter-role conflict occurs when an individual's different roles (for example, worker and parent) compete. Within the same role, competing or contradictory demands from different sources (for example, from separate departments or supervisors) may give rise to intra-role conflict.

Group Norms

Yet another clue to a group's structural type can be found in its norms or rules. Any course in organizational leadership must sensitize trainees to recognize and, if needed, reshape such norms. Whether explicit or implicit, norms tell group members how to behave in given situations. They have the positive effect of maintaining order, but they can also cause painful exclusion from the group. Newcomers who can't quickly grasp these rules may never be welcome. And seasoned members who violate group norms may be ignored, punished, or exiled. But if most of the group members ignore its norms, those rules no longer serve as a viable standard for behavior or affiliation, and will have to change if the group is to survive.

Examples of norms include how much socializing may occur at meetings; how group members dress at meetings; whether and when group members may go out together; whether meetings start on time or are reliably late; how much work members do; and how biting critical comments may be. Explicit or implicit, norms draw the border between acceptable and unacceptable actions within a collectivity. Naturally, each group member brings his or her own personal norms into the group, but these become influenced by other members and the collective purpose.

In a successful group, norms appropriate to their needs emerge and persist. Well-functioning norms facilitate group survival, make behavior more predictable, avoid embarrassing situations, and express shared values. Performance norms in particular determine how vigorously and productively individual members work. Of course, participants' performance norms may not accord with the manager's: Members who could perform at higher levels may choose not do so because of the group's performance norms. For example, workers may stop production 20 minutes before quitting time in order to wash up, yielding fewer items than management envisioned.

Reward-allocation norms determine how members are recognized for their effort or skill, and must be agreed to by a majority of the group. A norm of equality dictates identical treatment of all members: Every member contributes, so each reaps equal rewards. Equity norms insist that rewards be distributed according to each individual's contribution: Those who contribute most receive the largest rewards. Social responsibility norms grant benefits where they're most needed, so members with special hardships receive a larger share of the reward. The takeaway for your trainees: If emerging leaders demonstrate sensitivity to the values nourishing current norms in their industrial, commercial, or public organization, they will make more fitting executive decisions and will enjoy easier acceptance of any changes they must make in them.

Functional Classification of Groups and Member Roles

In addition to a group's structure, its level of functionality serves to categorize it. Glorious synergy or dreaded dysfunctions brand each group type and clarify for upcoming leadership how its efficacy could be maximized.

Group Cohesiveness

Many factors impact group togetherness. But it appears that the more exclusive the group—the harder it is to gain and retain membership—the more cohesive the group, because it's more identity-bound and because it's simply smaller. Groups also tend to solidify when they compete intensely with other groups, face a serious threat to survival, or spend a lot of time together.

Clearly, cohesive behavior in work groups has many benefits: worker satisfaction, low turnover and absenteeism, and high productivity. Indeed, evidence suggests that united groups typically outperform individuals when tasks require a variety of skills and experience. Such groups are flexible, quickly achieving a goal and moving on to the next. A vibrant esprit de corps motivates its excellent performance. In fact, since groups complete most of an organization's work, you can pretty accurately judge an organization's effectiveness by looking at the functionality of its groups. And as a business leadership developer, you can challenge your trainees to test this principle by observing organizations in the real world.

Ironically, though, too much cohesiveness threatens efficacy. It can interfere with productivity if the group spends more time interacting socially than working, or if specific group goals conflict with larger organizational goals. In addition, newcomers may have difficulty fitting into a group with a very high cohesion level.

Case in Point: Take the Lead

Occasionally, new trainees join a class well after it has started. I knew class members can get territorial about their favorite seats. But I was taken aback when some of the original cohort physically moved new-comers' books from desks and tried to exclude them from the seating arrangement. Although we resolved the immediate issue, terms like "my group" and "the outsiders" dogged the course all semester. I now appreciate that devoting a week or two to prepare for the change in group membership would have normalized it sooner and better.

Finally and worst of all, extremely cohesive groups are vulnerable to the psychological phenomenon of *groupthink*: group pressure (often unconscious) on individuals to always come to a consensus, however artificial. Groupthink rewards snap judgments and encourages poor decision-making behaviors like incomplete assessment of a problem, biased research and conclusions, automatic dismissal of alternative plans and views, and failure to examine the risks of the preferred choice. As a leadership instructor you'll want to alert trainees to the subtle symptoms of groupthink, and you can rest assured that facilitative leadership training will provide experiential knowledge of the hazards of exaggerated group loyalty.

Group Synergy

Group synergy occurs when the members' combined efforts exceed the sum of their individual efforts. Synergetic group behavior lets the group as a whole outperform even its best individual members working separately. In complete contrast to collectivities infected with groupthink, synergetic groups actively seek out points of disagreement and thus encourage fruitful discussion, while ineffective groups settle quickly, use primitive decision-making methods like averaging, and focus on task completion rather than finding the best solution.

Group Dysfunctions: Distractions, Factions, and Groupthink

Interestingly, you can teach emerging leaders as much about group types by examining unhealthy dynamics as by studying synergy, and you'll probably get a sampling of both in your class! Distractions draw individuals' attention away from the chosen group activity to an irrelevant one. They may stem from a group member's attentional disability, or the novelty of the distraction. Obvious examples include texting or surfing the web and going off topic in discussion.

Abraham Lincoln knew the hazards of another threat to group unity all too well, when he said "our own beloved country . . . is now afflicted with faction and civil war." Factions are sub-groups of individuals who splinter off from the original group into "parties within a party," or opposing power blocs within the main group. Unlike group-ordained subgroups, factions seek not to complete the collective mission, but to pursue a separate agenda by fragmenting the group into competing forces. Generally, a faction forms a cohesive, usually contentious minority that creates conflict within the whole group or organization.

If factions make group decisions impossible, we've seen that the dysfunction of groupthink shows that decisions made at any cost will be severely flawed. When group members prefer unanimity to honest appraisals of alternative solutions or minority views, their mental sharpness, reality-testing, and ethical judgment fail. Overly cohesive groups avoid seeking outside opinions; forgo constructive criticism; dismiss options out of hand; deny the possibility of failure and thus, any need for back-up plans; gather data selectively; share an illusion of invulnerability; believe unquestioningly in their own morality; rationalize poor decisions; share stereotypes; suppress expression of true feelings; and bully group members.

Even more hazardous, the dysfunctional dynamics of the "in group" ensures that its members overrate their own abilities in decision-making and underrate the abilities of their opponents—the "out group." So, not only would the opinions or complaints of marginalized group members, or members of a separate subgroup, be entirely ignored, but your views or guidance as a facilitator will also be ignored, because you are now the "out group" and part, or all, of the class is the "in group." Besides being unpleasant, such group rigidity makes it impossible for anyone—inside or outside the group—to practice real leadership.

Case in Point: Nip It in the Bud

Early in my career I learned the dangers of groupthink. In a course on strategic communications, the main goal of which was learning to communicate effectively as a leader, I was initially thrilled when the class seemed to coalesce almost instantly and enjoy their time together greatly. But as time went on I noticed that two class members were engaging in non-stop side conversations, and another was constantly on her cell phone, sometimes even leaving the room to answer a call. I approached one of the chatterers and suggested he change his seat as this behavior went against rules the group had adopted, but he refused to relocate, promising he would stop the side conversations.

Although the side conversations diminished, the other trainee remained on the phone, either texting or surfing the web so constantly it distracted me and her classmates. Finally I challenged the group as a whole, asking why they tolerated this disrespectful and disruptive behavior which flaunted their own norms. To my surprise, they defended their passivity, saying that they "tried to stop" the perpetrators, to no avail. I pointed out that this situation illustrated groupthink, lack of respect for themselves, and lack of leadership. Group members became highly defensive and angry at me, stating that it was my job to stop the behavior. This lesson taught me that uncorrected groupthink endangers not just individual trainees, but the whole class, me as a facilitator, and the entire enterprise of teaching leadership.

GROUP DYNAMICS IN YOUR CLASSROOM
Growing the Facilitative Classroom: Instructor and Learner Duties

Let's recall Tuckman's notion that as a group develops, it passes through predictable stages, beginning as a loose collection of persons and culminating as a cohesive collectivity. Each phase poses particular challenges to group members and leaders. Mastering the problematic feelings and behaviors that typically arise in each stage lets the group advance to the next one. In leadership development, this means that an organization follows a kind of natural maturation process that good executives encourage, but can't force. If we test Tuckman's five-stage model—forming, storming, norming, performing, adjourning—by applying it to the interactive leadership classroom, we find that it can identify positive group functions and potential dysfunctions as they appear. Equally valuable, it then shows us the appropriate ways you as an instructor, along with participants, may promote or fix them.

Stage 1: Forming

As the group's goals and leadership have not been established yet, this stage sees some uncertainty as well as budding relationships and group identity. This orientation period lets learners get acquainted, share expectations, and learn the group's purpose and rules. It resembles the group's practical and psychological birth, requiring learners to create group identity and loyalty, and to specify collective tasks. Commonly, learners at this point wonder about everything: why they are there, what they should do, and how they should do it. For this reason, dependence on the facilitator to provide structure, set goals, clarify values, and launch the mission will outweigh participants' interrelations. Despite its discomforts, the forming stage plants the trust and openness that will blossom in later stages, and should not be rushed—a useful point for facilitators and future executives to note.

Stage 1 Teaching Style: Instructor-Directed

A group in this phase requires clear statements of roles and goals, as well as basic information about the class agenda, deadlines, and requirements. Even in a facilitative setting, the instructor should allow himself or herself to be, however temporarily, the group's structural and emotional center.

Specific Instructor Responsibilities

Instructors should listen and mirror carefully, be available, maintain open communication and feedback channels, offer support and reassurance, keep group members on track, and establish behaviors and events that can become group traditions—everything a good leader would do in a young enterprise.

Specific Learner Responsibilities

Learners help the group-building process by getting to know one another, accepting their new identity as group members, and learning the group's purpose. How well each candidate does these tasks will give you an initial hint about their readiness to lead—at least, at this point in their evolution.

Stage 2: Storming

Resistance, negativity, ambiguity, and conflict over authority characterize this phase. It challenges group members to foster good communication by expressing feelings productively, tolerating disagreement, and avoiding shattering into factions. The good news for you is that confrontations occur among group members or with the instructor now because learners feel comfortable enough to protest and to exert their own power. But without constructive strategies to help members move from conflict to commitment, some participants may isolate and thereby damage group cohesion.

Stage 2 Teaching Style: Coaching

While groups in this stage still require directive supervision they also need a push toward eventual independence. As the facilitator, you'll serve not only as a mediator of disputes but also as a teacher of group norms and values. You'll need to hear, identify, and summarize problems; manage conflicts; encourage participation; provide recognition; and build group-wide alliances.

Specific Instructor Responsibilities

At this stage you as the facilitator need to provide answers, answers, and more answers! Repeat key information often; set short-term goals; restate mission, objectives, and priorities; and create opportunities for participation.

Specific Learner Responsibilities

Because the group will experience its greatest conflicts over goals and power during the storming stage, members must consciously focus on their commonalities. Individuals often vie for leadership during this stage of development, and someone may appoint himself or herself a "leader," albeit without having real leadership skills. If the leadership claim is not universally and permanently accepted—and it rarely is—the group may freeze into an ineffective existence, never maturing to later stages. Resolving the risks of this stage may require your leadership.

Stage 3: Norming

Having conquered competition, the group process now demonstrates cooperation and fellowship, and collective effort starts to show real, positive results. The current task is to channel the skills, energy, and growing interdependence of group members into coordinated work. People begin to experience unity, start to share ideas and feelings, give and solicit feedback, and explore information and strategies related to tasks at hand. As members realize they feel good being part of the group, they briefly abandon their assigned (and even self-assigned) goals, and indulge in a period of play—the enjoyment of cohesive group life.

Stage 3 Teaching Style: Learner-Directed With Facilitator Support

Group members now understand their roles and aims and are willing to work at them. So you as the leadership facilitator should push group members to become less dependent on your authority, while still providing support to coordinate participants' efforts.

Specific Instructor Responsibilities

Keep participants focused and communication channels open, aim for universal participation, translate organizational goals into group projects, delegate decisions to the group, and promote creative thinking.

Specific Participant Responsibilities

At this point, class members need to master skills for shared projects and to become increasingly interdependent by removing the leader from the center of every decision. To answer this challenge, participants should try to discover colleagues' unique talents, designate responsibilities among them, and decide how to evaluate collective progress.

Stage 4: Performing

Productivity, autonomy, unity, and commitment now characterize the group, which has grown into a collective organism mightier than the sum of its parts. Like a wise executive, you've nurtured your "company" so interdependent group members work well alone, in subgroups, or together; display energy and enthusiasm; and often sacrifice individual gain (power, praise) for the sake of the group's performance. Well-defined group tasks rely on joint rather than individual action. Freed of the fear that their mistakes will lead to finger-pointing or power grabs, group members engage in free-ranging brainstorming and experimentation to solve problems.

Stage 4 Teaching Style: Participant-Directed With Mentoring

Because groups in this phase have set their own rules and become energized by their achievements, the instructor should serve as an ambassador or philosopher and allow group members to run the day-to-day business.

Specific Instructor Responsibilities

Facilitators must provide resources, remove obstacles, reward high performance and interaction, and celebrate successes.

Specific Participant Responsibilities

In a cohesive, mature, performing group, members take on the group's business and let you, the facilitator, operate mostly on the sidelines. Now individuals accept one another, resolve conflicts through group discussion, and make decisions through a group-wide process focused on relevant goals rather than individuals' emotional issues (such as power plays or attention-getting).

Stage 5: Adjourning

Once your class attains this stage, you'll all feel a sense of successful closure. Its object completed, or its membership altered by graduation, promotion, or new recruitment, this leadership development group's process ends. Personal relations will be disengaged and tasks will be terminated. Group members (and the instructor) often experience both pride and sadness as they prepare to disband. Of course, permanent or constantly renewed groups do not experience this stage of development as a collectivity, although departing individuals may. In those groups, this stage marks a new group's formation.

Stage 5 Teaching Style: Participant-Directed

This ultimate stage requires the instructor to jog the group's memory and activate its hopes by reminding participants how far they've come both collectively and individually, and encouraging continuing development.

Specific Instructor Responsibilities

Through asking participants to assess the course both informally in class and through anonymous evaluations, you as the facilitator model openness to critique and appreciation of your trainees' growth. Course evaluations should do more than let learners grade you and the class. They should help participants clarify their understanding of their own success and track their transformation throughout the course. That means that assessment mechanisms should measure how well your course instilled the group's ethical values of integrity, initiative, and respect for self and others. Further, as we saw in this book's first chapter, adult education theory supports learner-centered instruction, which includes emotional as well as intellectual growth, self-directed education, use of life experience, and application of new knowledge to real life. So your evaluation instruments should measure how well the course achieved all those teaching ideals. (For guidance, check out Part II and the Appendix on surveying leadership trainees and their superiors.) Last but not least, you as the instructor can remain accessible by establishing an alumni blog for group graduates and by offering letters of recommendation to help in their future endeavors.

Specific Participant Responsibilities

Participants should fill out course evaluations as completely and honestly as possible, for their own benefit and that of future leadership candidates. In addition, they can strengthen their pride in their collective accomplishments by sharing recollections of their best and worst class moments, and bid farewell to colleagues with a few encouraging or appreciative words about each. As they know each other well now, participants may wish to give themselves a graduation party or distribute prizes celebrating classmates' contributions, merits, or characteristics—best practices described at length in Part III. They should also take up the instructor's invitation to write in the alumni blog!

How Facilitators Teach Leadership

Practical Ethics: Integrity, Initiative, and Respect for Self and Others

As noted in the previous chapter, good facilitators demonstrate the same principles of integrity, initiative, and respect for self and others that they want their trainees to show. So, interestingly, the best practical advice available to facilitative instructors—and to participants as they learn to lead—supports those same moral virtues shown in Table 3.1.

Table 3.1

Show integrity (commit to principles).	Show initiative (energy and creativity).	Show respect for self and others.
Center yourself and be reflective as you teach.	Use and stimulate goal-oriented thinking and behavior.	Listen to others actively, not passively, by mirroring their comments.
Tell the truth as you see it, but correct and enlarge your views.	Structure cooperative rather than competitive relationships.	Elicit everyone's ideas.
Use reason and logic, but let your principles and ideals guide your speech and actions.	Encourage cooperation by demonstrating it.	Challenge others' ideas in order to strengthen them rather than to dismantle them.
To stay trustworthy, keep your promises and don't move the goal posts.	Build synergy by knowing and valuing the talents of each group member.	Be gentle in critique but firm in conviction.
	Show learners how much they can influence their present and their future.	Foster a classroom culture that respects each member's contribution.

		Build participants' trust in you by being trustworthy, so they can trust each other.
	Be positive and practical.	
	Stay flexible to take advantage of unplanned "teachable moments" to impart information or insights.	Confront conflicts as a group instead of avoiding them or imposing solutions.
		Seek to resolve conflicts with win/win strategies.

Assessing Group Dynamics

As we know from chapter 2, content and process (also called dynamics) are the two constant ingredients in all human interactions. Content—the subject matter or task—gets plenty of attention. But process—what happens between group members—gets short shrift, even though snags in it produce almost all the problems groups can face. Process involves morale, competition, cooperation, and conflict. Awareness of group process lets you as the facilitator and, eventually, your candidates diagnose and fix these issues promptly.

Group Dynamics Worksheet

This section offers you guidelines on what to observe in class-wide group and subgroup behavior and gives you a convenient worksheet to duplicate. Fill it out immediately after each or every other class session, so you can focus completely on the class process and trainees don't feel uncomfortable or "spied on."

Participation and Membership

Participation in group discussion and projects usually requires the sense of belonging known as membership, but some may feel connected to the group without participating.

- Do you notice early arrivals and late departures (eagerness to spend time together), or late arrivals and early departures?

  _____

  _____

- What are the greeting and parting behaviors? Do they bond the group?

  _____

  _____

- Does everyone seem equally welcome? If not, who's most welcome? Least?

  _____

  _____

- Who are the high participators? Who are the low participators?

  _____

  _____

- Do you see any shift in participation, such as high participators becoming quiet or low participators speaking up? If so, why?

  _____

  _____

- How are silent people treated? How is their silence interpreted?

  _____

  _____

- Who keeps the ball rolling? Why?

  _____

  _____

- Are there "in" and "out" groups? What qualities distinguish each? Who is in each? How are "in-group" and "out-group" people treated?

  _____

  _____

- Is there informal voluntary (not assigned) subgrouping? Who's in the subgroups?

  _____

  _____

Influence

Influence differs from participation. Some people speak little but capture the group's attention, while others talk a lot but are rarely heeded.

- Which group members are high in influence? Which are low in influence?

  _____

  _____

- Are there shifts in influence? What do you think caused the shift?

  _____

  _____

- Do you see rivalry in the group? If so, what effect does it have on members?

  _____

  _____

Communication

One of the most telling, but in fact the easiest, aspect of group process to observe is its communication pattern.

- Who talks? For how long? How often?

  _____

  _____

- Whom do people speak to? (Potential supporters? The whole group? No one at all?)

  _____

  _____

- Who talks after whom?

  _____

  _____

- Who interrupts whom?

  _____

  _____

- What types of communication are used (statements, questions, tones of voice, facial expressions, sounds, or gestures)?

  _____

  _____

Decision-Making

Groups and individuals display a range of decision-making mechanisms. Some try to impose decisions on the group, while others seek consensus.

- Does anyone make a decision (for example, pick a discussion topic) and act on it without checking with other group members? What effect does this behavior have on members?

  _____

  _____

- Who supports another group member's suggestions? Does this support result in the two members deciding for the whole group? How does this affect other members?

  _____

  _____

- When faced with making a decision, does the group drift off topic? If so, who topic-jumps? Why do the group's discussions get scattered?

  _____

  _____

- Does a majority push a decision over a minority's objections? Does the group always call for a vote and follow the "majority rules" idea?

  _____

  _____

- Does anyone try to get all group members to weigh in on a decision?

  _____

  _____

- Does anyone try to force a consensus? If so, why? What happens?

  _____

  _____

- Does anyone make contributions that are totally ignored? If so, why?

  _____

  _____

Work Dynamics and Maintenance Functions

Judge who keeps the ball rolling.

- Are behaviors focused on the task at hand?

  _____

  _____

- Does anyone goad the group to stay on task?

  _____

  _____

- Who gets others involved in discussions?

  _____

  _____

- Who cuts others off?

  _____

  _____

- Does anyone try to summarize what has been said in the group?

  _____

  _____

- Is anyone asking for facts, ideas, feelings, feedback, or alternatives?

  _____

  _____

- How well do group members express their ideas?

  _____

  _____

- How are group members' ideas rejected?

  _____

  _____

- Does anyone try to integrate everyone's ideas, even if contradictory?

  _____

  _____

- Is there a peacemaker? Does that member use objective (content-based) problem-solving techniques, try to pacify emotions, or both?

  _____

  _____

Atmosphere

Class members' "chemistry" sets the emotional tone of the group.

- Does the atmosphere encourage work, play, apathy, or anger?

  _____

  _____

- Is the emotional climate of the group/subgroup friendly or cold?

  _____

  _____

- Do you observe "body language" signs of anger, frustration, irritation, friendship, or boredom?

  _____

  _____

- Does anyone attempt to suppress conflict or unpleasantness? Does anyone foster them?

  _____

  _____

- Are group members overly polite to one another? Are only positive feelings ever expressed? Do some group members consistently avoid giving any negative feedback?

  _____

  _____

- Do you see any attempts to block the expression of intense feelings? How is this done? How does it affect group members?

  _____

  _____

- Do group members feel free to ask each other about feelings, or are questions restricted to intellectual topics or events outside the classroom experience?

  _____

  _____

- Do particular members provoke or annoy others? Does anyone in the group observe or comment on them? How does such notice affect members?

_____

_____

Norms

Some norms are helpful, but some may be harmful.

- Do you notice participation norms such as turn-taking or limiting the length of comments?

_____

_____

- Are there norms concerning the kinds of topics allowed, such as "no personal stuff" or "no religion or politics"?

_____

_____

- Do group members restrict their own behaviors as agreed (turning off phones, not reading during discussion, or not using insulting language)?

_____

_____

- Do group members consciously abide by established codes of conduct, such as confirming that they understood a previous comment before objecting to it?

_____

_____

Adjusting Group Dynamics

Your observation of the above processes will probably reveal some problematic behaviors both in individuals and the group. Let's explore the causes, and some effective cures, for each of these.

Dysfunctional Individual Behaviors

Although they're often connected, dysfunctional behaviors by individuals can be classified as disregarding group norms, "checking out," or disrespecting people—exactly the opposite of the integrity, initiative, and respect for self and others that you as a facilitator exercise and encourage.

Table 3.2

Disregarding group norms	"Checking out" of the group experience	Disrespecting other people
• Coming late to class and disrupting it • Avoiding group-determined responsibilities • Ignoring rules for turn-taking, discussion, work, or other behaviors	• Withholding reactions, feelings, or information • Texting or web-surfing • Focusing, on side issues (nitpicking) or jumping off topic • Engaging in side conversations during group discussion or activities	• Cutting off other's comments • Attacking people rather than issues • Dominating discussion • Attention-seeking

Recall that badly behaved group members have taken on blocking roles for reasons—often unconscious—that are wholly separate from the aims of the group. Your role as a facilitator is to help them transform into functional group members, so they can progress to become effective leaders. Of course, difficult participants generally resist or struggle with reflection and reform—that's why they're difficult. But your skill at identifying unhealthy dynamics, plumbing their causes, and responding with patient firmness can adjust the group process.

Silent, talkative, or just plain nasty participants all threaten the feeling of comfort essential to group learning. It's natural for an instructor to react with irritation toward them, but it's disastrous for several reasons: It removes focus from the group, ignores the root of the problem and therefore its solution, and, worst of all, models poor leadership. Vilifying troublesome learners neither helps them improve nor reins them in, and further damages the group process by wasting an opportunity for you to demonstrate ethical and effective management. Your first step to manage the problem is to understand the offender.

A participant may disengage in a facilitative setting because of shyness, personal troubles, intellectual insecurity (often disguised as claims of superiority), or a habit of relying on external authority. Encourage reluctant speakers by making eye contact and asking yes-or-no questions, acknowledging any contribution the participant makes and requesting more details, or giving the participant practice speaking up by summarizing discussions in less intimidating subgroups. You may also ask him or her, in private, why he or she is so quiet.

A talkative participant may wish to flaunt an extensive vocabulary or body of knowledge. Paradoxically similar to the silent member, such an individual may actually feel unequal to the course demands. Either way, you should remind the whole group of time limits, briefly restate the speaker's points and the agenda, ask the participant to explain the relevance of his or her comments, or, again, speak to the participant privately. Participants indulging in side conversations may also feel shame about not understanding the topic or may fear that their contributions will be criticized or ignored, and be seeking a helpful ally. Still, you can quash these disruptions by requesting side-conversationalists to share their ideas, asking if they would like to start a new topic for general review, or repeating a point made in the general discussion and soliciting their opinions.

A highly argumentative or aggressive participant may have psychological problems, lack social skills, be upset by open debate on topics he or she considers sacred, or feel—rightly or wrongly—slighted by the group or the facilitator. Appropriate solutions you can apply include focusing strictly on the content of the trainee's comments, restating his or her words more diplomatically, opening up the discussion from the aggressor's "target" to the entire group, or tabling the comments for the next meeting. If these on-site fixes don't lower tensions you will have to talk to the trainee privately. And if the behavior persists, let the participant know that no one is permitted to jeopardize the group agenda and environment, and he or she may be dropped from the course.

This option is a last resort, particularly if trainees are attending a mandatory course. Occasionally just the fact that a class has been mandated elicits resentment, boredom, and flouting of basic social norms. Resentful people block out the speaker, often literally, with crossed arms and legs; others telegraph their lack of interest by shuffling papers or grooming their nails. Still others loudly claim, "I don't engage in that behavior," "That never happens anymore," "We've all gone through this training a million times," or even, "What makes you such an expert?"

Mandatory training goals are most likely to be met—and resentment avoided—when organizations first frame their purpose in a way that elicits employee support. But not all organizations perform this preparatory step, so you as the facilitator may need to fill it in. You may have to reinforce the obligatory nature of the task and the chain of command that decided on it. Still, you must listen respectfully to the complaints (even if they're not always respectful), acknowledge them, and reassure the participants that they will be heard. With very few exceptions in many years of teaching, once I validate their concerns and demonstrate my genuine interest in them, I am usually thanked and am often asked questions one-on-one after the training. As in all facilitation, the key to your success is building a relationship of mutual trust and respect.

Dysfunctional Group Behaviors

Problematic group processes can come not just from difficult individuals but from the operation of the group as a whole or a subgroup. We already discussed a prime example of collective dysfunction, groupthink, in which all members suppress their doubts and creativity in favor of an artificial unanimity. But as a savvy facilitator you can remedy even this general plague by fostering healthy, constructive conflict. Try dividing group members into competing subgroups; inviting outside experts to present in class; or appointing some group members to function as a devil's advocate to challenge group ideas.

Lencioni (2002) identifies five common dysfunctions most participants, and thus most groups, struggle with: unwillingness to be vulnerable, fear of conflict, lack of commitment, avoidance of accountability, and inattention to results. He notes that these difficulties are interrelated. Interestingly, we can also see that all of these dysfunctions in fact cascade, one by one, from an original absence of trust among group members. Without trust, participants resist opening themselves up to group scrutiny and critique, they fear critique as causing conflict and therefore censor themselves, they lack commitment because they censored self-expression, they feel no accountability for group goals they never committed to, and they don't care about results because their own interests outweigh those of a group they never truly joined.

But if you create a safe environment by taking the first (and continuing) steps to demonstrate trustworthiness, group members will feel able to expose their weaknesses, seek help from others and offer help to others, accept responsibility, risk argument, applaud and employ each other's skills, focus on collective aims rather than power struggles, identify and fix snags in group interrelations, move through tasks efficiently, and enjoy exciting work together.

To establish trust, you as a leadership facilitator must (in addition to the techniques in the previous chapter) constantly demonstrate your integrity, initiative, and respect for self and others. And when faced with individual or group dysfunction, take action so you can help the group balance the equal aims of universal participation and fulfilling the group agenda.

Case in Point: It Has to Sink in

Fairly recently I had a class member learn cooperative leadership the hard way. With unusually poor interpersonal skills, he scotched his sub-group's grade by presenting points other members had nixed, ignored classmates' contributions, declared himself "a brilliant leader," and called colleagues his "followers." So when I solicited group feedback on everyone's executive skills, he reacted with shock when no one even noticed his self-acclaimed leadership—in fact, someone bluntly asked him, "If there are no followers, how could you be a leader?"

More dramatically, in a suicide-prevention exercise with guest speakers from the LAPD SWAT, he escalated the risks to the "suicide" character so gravely that others had to intervene. When participants tried to explain his missteps, he laughed and sauntered out of the room.

I thought I'd never see him again. But he came by my office the next day and asked nervously if he was still enrolled. When I assured him he was, his relief and the gratitude he expressed, shamefaced, for everyone's guidance stunned me. Throughout the rest of the course, his increasingly respectful listening and consulting showed what he was learning experientially: Only by empowering the group can one become an effective leader. And I learned experientially not to give up too soon on the profoundly transformative effects of interactive education.

THE MEDIUM IS THE MESSAGE
The Facilitator as Leader: Modeling Ethical and Effective Leadership

Facilitative training in leadership requires you to enable both learning about leadership and practicing leadership. That is, you motivate and empower learners to lead by delegating increasingly complex tasks to individuals and the group as a whole. Thus your facilitative classroom functions both as a laboratory for studying leadership and a gym for exercising it.

By refereeing the group process you can keep individuals from interrupting or dominating others, and convey acceptance of everyone's equal value. Playing the part of a neutral party with an open, pragmatic view of all points raised, you're the even-handed encourager, observer, and adjuster of group dynamics rather than the judge of content.

As discussed, facilitative leadership training is transformational and provokes emotionally powerful, often deeply discomforting experiences. Yet classes are not therapeutic groups and you are not a therapist. In fact, one of the highest ethical demands placed on you as a facilitator is ensuring that neither you nor any group member crosses a participant's psychological boundary. But because failing this ideal is so easy—and so attractive to the unscrupulous—libertarians, "grass roots" theorists, and organizational development consultants have questioned the morality of transformational leadership itself (Bass and Steidlmeier 1999).

We can extend their concerns about transformational leadership to interactive leadership training. Indeed, for both leadership and facilitative teaching to be genuine—to be generous instead of selfish—they must grow from an ethical foundation. Examining the four components of transformational leadership that Bass and Steidlmeier identified—idealized influence, inspirational motivation, intellectual stimulation, and individualized consideration—we can imagine these elements being manipulated to counterfeit honest transformation. (Or we can just remember history!) Clearly the sincerity of your concern for trainees, your values, group members' freedom to question your ideas, and the morality of the actions you and your candidates pursue, form the criteria of your training's truly transformative power.

Participant Practice of Ethical and Effective Leadership

If you as a facilitator have brought the group to function with integrity, initiative, and respect for self and others, participants themselves come to demonstrate excellent leadership. They hold themselves accountable for assigned work, spur on unenthusiastic performers, manage conflict constructively, recognize and repair problems without blaming, and debate with verve and honesty to arrive at the common good of completing the agenda. Recall that you don't know everything and don't have to. Model modesty, and teach the central truth that true leaders constantly educate themselves. In the end, you'll find that you've taught leadership by being an ethical and effective leader yourself.

SUMMARY

Facilitator modeling and participant practice turns learners into leaders. The crucial role of trust in facilitative training of leaders proves that the equation of effective and ethical leadership, far from being an empty ideal, is a fact. For only the experience of the interactive instructor's ethical relationship with, and protective support of, individuals allows them to coalesce into a healthy group. And only in a healthy group can they practice leading with safety, responsibility, ingenuity, and enjoyment.

Your character, words, and behavior teach more than any leadership textbook ever could. Once you as a teacher unleash the power of ethical relationships within your class, trainees feel the sense of trust that fosters openness, creativity, innovation, accountability, cohesion, and camaraderie. The ethical underpinning of that transformative experience is what makes facilitation so superlatively able to turn learners into leaders.

REFLECTION AND NEXT STEPS

1. **Think back on your own experiences in organizations.** Have you ever felt marginalized or ganged-up on in a group? Did the leader, or another group member, step in to refocus the group more productively? How did this make you feel about the organization?

2. **Reflect on the connection between morals and management.** How does the idea that effective leadership teaching requires ethical teachers challenge or strengthen your views on educating leaders?

3. **Consider how different types of organizations encourage different individual behaviors.** In what ways might competition within an organization conflict with cooperation? How can the leader get the best of both—creativity and camaraderie—from a group?

REFERENCES AND RESOURCES

Bass, B., and P. Steidlmeier. (1999). "Ethics, Character, and Authentic Transformational Leadership." *The Leadership Quarterly*, 10(2): 181-217.

Beal, D., R. Cohen, M. Burke, and C. McLendon. (December, 2003). "Cohesion and Performance in Groups: A Meta-Analytic Clarification of Construct Relations." *Journal of Applied Psychology*, 88(6): 989-1004.

Beck, A., and C. Lewis. (2000). *The Process of Group Psychotherapy: Systems for Analyzing Change*. Washington, D.C.: American Psychological Association.

Creighton, T. (2005). *Leading From Below the Surface: A Non-Traditional Approach to School Leadership*. Thousand Oaks, CA: Corwin Press.

Eisenberg, J. (2007). Group Cohesiveness. In Baumeister, R.F., and K.D. Vohs (editors), *Encyclopaedia of Social Psychology*. Thousand Oaks, CA: SAGE.

Forsyth, D. (2010). *Group Dynamics*, 5th edition. Belmont, CA: Wadsworth.

Hartman, J., and G. Gibbard. (1974). "Anxiety, Boundary Evolution and Social Change." In Gibbard, G.S., J. Hartman, and R.D. Mann (editors), *Analysis of Groups*. San Francisco: Jossey-Bass.

Homans, G. (1974). *Social Behaviour: Its Elementary Forms,* revised edition. New York: Harcourt Brace Jovanovich.

Huczynski, A., D. Buchanan, and R. Dunham. (2007). *Organizational Behavior: An Introductory Text*. Upper Saddle River, NJ: Prentice Hall.

Janis, I. (1972). *Victims of Groupthink: A Psychological Study of Foreign-Policy Decisions and Fiascoes*, 2nd edition. Boston: Houghton Mifflin.

Lencioni, P. (2002). *The Five Dysfunctions of a Team*. San Francisco: Jossey-Bass.

Levinger, G. (2010). "Ringelmann Effect." In Levine, J.M., and M.A. Hogg (editors) *Encyclopedia of Group Processes and Intergroup Relations*. Thousand Oaks, CA: SAGE Publications.

Luthans, F. (2005). *Organizational Behavio*r. New York: McGraw-Hill.

McFadzean, E., and A. O'Loughlin. (2000). "Five Strategies for Improving Group Effectiveness." *Strategic Change,* 9:103-114.

Mueller, J. (2012). "Why Individuals in Larger Teams Perform Worse." *Organizational Behavior and Human Decision Processes*, 117(1): 111-124.

Robbins, S., and T. Judge. (2012). *Organizational Behavior*, 15th edition. Boston: Prentice Hall.

Schein, E. (2004). *Organizational Culture and Leadership*. San Francisco: Jossey-Bass.

Singh, A., and N. Muncherji. (February, 2007). "Team Effectiveness and its Measurement: A Framework." *Global Business Review*, 8(1): 119-133.

Smith, R. (May, 2005). "Working With Difference in Online Collaborative Groups." *Education Quarterly*, 55(3): 182-199.

Tucker, B., and F. Russell. (Spring, 2004). "The Influence of the Transformational Leader." *Journal of Leadership and Organizational Studie*s, 10(4): 103-111.

Tuckman, B. (1965). "Developmental Sequences in Small Groups." *Psychological Bulletin*, 63:384-389.

Wheelan, S. (2010). *Creating Effective Teams: A Guide for Members and Leaders*, 3rd edition. Los Angeles: SAGE.

Knowledge@Wharton. (June, 2006). "Is Your Team Too Big? Too Small? What's the Right Number?" June 14, http://knowledge.wharton.upenn.edu/article.cfm?articleid=1501 (accessed July 22, 2013).

Yalom, I., and M. Leszcz. (2005). *The Theory and Practice of Group Psychotherapy,* 5th edition. New York: Basic Books.

PART II

BEYOND ANECDOTE: MEASURING THE EFFECTIVENESS OF FACILITATIVE TRAINING

Chapter 4

Facilitative Training in the Private Sector

This chapter covers:

- why and how you can apply public sector leadership development successes to the private sector

- measuring the effectiveness of the facilitative training of leaders in any sector

- advantages business organizations have in measuring the success of facilitative training.

EVALUATION OF LEADERSHIP TRAINING IN THE PRIVATE SECTOR

The private sector, meaning any for-profit enterprise not funded by government (public) funds, has long recognized the value of leadership training to ready mid-level managers for executive positions. It's also been quick to grasp the merits of facilitative training of leaders for team-building and innovation. Given these facts, research on the efficacy of facilitative (or any) executive education in the business world is surprisingly scarce. While scores of leadership scholars and business advisors have jumped on the facilitation bandwagon, similar numbers have decried the total absence of any objective proof or explanation of its success. So until facilitative training for private sector leadership receives real scrutiny—perhaps through a survey such as that in the next chapter on public service employees—you'll have to apply to the private sphere what's been proven about facilitation in public sector leadership programs.

Luckily, having read the previous chapter, you can do this with complete confidence, because you know two essential points about group dynamics in the facilitative classroom: First, every group (business or non-profit) creates its own culture; and, second, facilitative teaching actually requires adjustment to a group's specific culture. So to help you apply all you've learned about dynamics in different groups and how facilitation adjusts to them, we'll first practice by identifying, and then fine-tuning for, differences between the two main spheres of our economy, the private and the public.

PRIVATE AND PUBLIC SECTOR ORGANIZATIONAL CULTURES

In both economic sectors, the effectiveness of facilitative executive education depends on the same elements: instructors, participants, and organizations. But business employees and organizations may have significantly different motivations and systems for advancing leadership skills than public servants and organizations. These varying ends and means stem from the dissimilar cultures of each—what we might call the corporate and the civic.

Motivations and Methods for Leadership Development

Personal and Organizational Motivations in Private Enterprise and Public Service

Even without quantitative research, it's a fair guess that midlevel managers in private sector organizations pursue leadership training both for personal growth and for promotion. The fact that leadership coursework can earn them a promotion illustrates that organizations have their own motivation for supporting those of trainees. (See Part I, chapter 1 on the ability of facilitative leadership education to integrate individual and organizational interests.) As we'll see more explicitly in the next chapter, most law enforcement officers and public safety personnel also enroll in leadership degree programs for the same double impetus: to hone personal skills and to advance in rank. And there, too, such advancement proves their department's interest in candidate's training.

However, there are motivational differences between the two sectors. While advancement in public-sphere employment certainly requires very hard-won attainments (advanced degrees, good work reviews, seniority), at a certain point basic job security is generally greater than it is in the business world. This greater surety may let public servants pursue leadership positions more for personal ambition and interest, rather than from any urgent sense that their jobs are hanging in the balance. Thus they may approach leadership training with less stress about their relative standing in the class than participants in the private sector. Put differently, in the private sphere an individual's motivations for engaging in leadership development may be more practical—perhaps even enforced from above—than the reasons for which public service employees pursue leadership education. Greater job insecurity in private enterprise may impose greater pressure on executive candidates than is generally found among public sector course enrollees. As the facilitator of future business leaders, then, you would want to get a sense of how truly interactive, open, and cohesive you can make your executive training course if each individual trainee's financial advance—or, sometimes, survival—hinges on it.

Training Methods in Private Enterprise and Public Service

As Senge (2000) reminds us, if motivations for leadership education differ according to the organizational context (its structure, policies, and general culture), its preferred style of leadership education and its openness to learning varies as well. Leading and learning styles do not differ from one organization to another; Higgs and Dulewicz (2002) note that they may also fluctuate dynamically within the same organization as it evolves new policies, changes management, or re-orients itself in the market. So to be an able facilitator you must, first, grasp these dynamic elements of an organization's educational aims, and then adjust the design of your training to accommodate them.

Accommodating Organizational Cultures: The Strength of Facilitation

We saw that facilitative leadership training can function well in nearly all institutional settings if—as intended—its design accommodates each setting's organizational culture. The corporate culture of individual competitiveness—the motor of the American private sector—may inadvertently limit its ability and desire to encourage interactive, cooperative, participant-led group functioning. Certainly, plenty of perfectly capitalist corporations here and in Western Europe think that a more communal approach—partial ownership and control by workers, family-friendly schedules, mentoring for beginning employees— provides a more successful business model. And many companies have done extremely well for themselves following that paradigm. But it's still the case that a corporation's decision whether to adopt liberal workplace policies or to keep the traditional American top-down structure will shape the type of facilitative training it wants for its executives. And the type of leadership education it wants in turn will impact the design of any interactive leadership program you offer.

For instance, as seen earlier, facilitative leadership development programs for law enforcement personnel required that the instructor recognize, confront, and utilize the particularities of their institutional culture—habits of respecting authority and repressing emotionality—which worked as sources of resistance. In fact, when the facilitator acknowledged those aspects of police culture without shaming candidates, it became easier for the trainees themselves to recognize, and to transcend, those habits. In the public sector context, then, facilitative trainers need to anticipate participants' reluctance to lead by themselves, as well as their tendency toward groupthink. As a specific example, facilitative instructors of police officers, especially at first, had to stimulate internal group debate and goad participants to voice independent opinions based on their own experience and knowledge, since the practice of welcoming conflicting views was relatively under exercised in law enforcement organizational culture. But when the facilitator was able to harness public service candidates' professional interest in improving their communication skills both inside the department and in the communities they serve, the trainees rose to the challenge. (To review groupthink see Part I, chapter 3.)

When you take on the task of educating businesspeople in executive arts—what we've been calling leadership skills—you'll probably be going for the exact opposite effect, compared to facilitators of public service trainees! But the principle's the same: You as the facilitator must acknowledge and utilize the specificities of each organization's culture. For example, although different companies exhibit an identifiable organizational style to varying degrees and at different stages of their growth, most private sector enterprises share at least one classic trait—in general, they tend to value individual drive over group cohesion. The deeply ingrained free-market view that competition produces the best outcome—survival of the marketplace fittest—may appear to conflict with the cooperative and interactive orientation of facilitation. So your task as a facilitative leadership instructor in this cultural context will be to encourage cooperative, joint creativity and mutual support within a business mindset—no easy task, but one you'll pick up with the following tips.

Taking Trainees From Cut-Throat to Cooperative—but Still Capitalist

As a leadership facilitator in corporate settings, then, you need to reorient ingrained habits of individual rivalry to the benefit of the group—exactly what's expected of a business leader. You might start doing this by employing teaching techniques tailored to increasing camaraderie and cooperativeness. For example, perhaps you'll configure subgroups in the class as though they were contending individuals by assigning (or, better, eliciting) team names, cheers, and "uniforms" (which may be as simple as team-specific colored paper wristbands). Another technique shows how competitiveness can serve communal aims: Challenge participants to strive against themselves and to produce a "personal best" presentation or project for the class. Yet another method in your arsenal for transforming self-interestedness into collective interest has you set up Cooperation Contests that reward individuals for efforts that support their whole group—or maybe even help a "rival" one!

Now you've gotten some useful tips on applying the principles of group dynamics, the techniques of interactive education, and the transformative quality of facilitative training of leaders in the realm of private enterprise. Most likely, you've been convinced, like most researchers in business leadership studies, that facilitation has unmatched power to develop effective leaders in the private sector. Next question is, how can businesses know if it's working?

Research on the Effectiveness of Facilitative Leadership Training in the Private Sector

Leading scholars in the field of private-sector leadership, including luminaries such as Heifetz, Linsky, Jenkins, Johnstone, Fern, Kegan, Lahey, Parks, Singh,

Munchergi, and Yi, hail from the business community itself or from business think-tanks. And, as we saw, they champion facilitation with near unanimity as the optimal approach for executive development. It would certainly stand to reason, then, that the private sector would have pretty universally adopted this technique in managerial training. Surprisingly and unfortunately, no quantitative research confirms this logical assumption.

It follows that, despite business theorists' hands-down favoring of facilitation as an executive training tool and its presumably widespread use in the business community, currently there is no quantitative and precious little other evidence on its effectiveness (there's none on its use). More than 40 years of researching business leadership and several decades of calling for a facilitative approach to promoting it have yielded no studies on the value of the facilitative teaching of leaders. In fact, notwithstanding the overwhelming agreement among business educators backing facilitative techniques for all business subjects (including but not limited to leadership), most courses still rely primarily on top-down, teacher-led discussion. Although Jenkins's (2012) surveys teaching techniques including role play and experiential learning, his research finds them rarely employed and does not measure their effectiveness. Given ASTD's estimate that U.S. organizations spent nearly $164.2 billion on employee learning and development in 2012 alone, it's clear that some objective measurement of teaching effectiveness would be in order (Miller and Mandzuk 2013).

One explanation for this assessment gap may be that exploring even the basic question, "what is business leadership?"—what Hales (1986) called "good" or "bad" managerial practice—has also produced little accord. Scholars such as Avolio, Bass, Jung, Barker, House, Aditya, Kim, Yuki, and Axelsson squabble over the fundamental definition of effectual leadership or accuse each other of irrelevance to the private sector. Some, like Bennis, Collins, House, Aditya, Thompson, Stuart, and Lindsay, assert that good business leadership does in fact demonstrate specific and universal qualities. But Collingwood, Goffee,

Jones, Higgs, Rowland, R. Hogan, J. Hogan, Kaiser, Kouznes, and Posner specify that the small number of skill or competence areas needed for good leadership essentially boil down to the leader's personality—what Goffee and Jones (2002) refer to as "being yourself, with skill." Still other studies, such as those of Kets de Vries and Florent-Treacy (2002), specify that leadership qualities, although they can't be measured, can be analyzed as a combination of behavioral, cognitive, and personality factors, one of which is the leader's own ability to learn.

The one item all these thinkers do acknowledge, though, is that there's very sparse empirical evidence supporting the efficacy of any specific executive quality. In fact, numerous researchers (Bass, Avolio, Fiedler, Flanagan, Spurgeon, Garavan, McQuire, Hersey, Blanchard, Higgs, Rowland, Jaworski, Senge, and Wheatley) even deny the existence of any universal managerial virtues at all, and argue the contingency theory—that leadership effectiveness is so context-specific it can be defined only situationally, on a case-by-case basis.

Leadership studies on the private sector seem to be approaching a consensus that there is no consensus about executive performance or qualities—and, therefore, on how to teach them. At best, authors including Goffee, Jones, Higgs, and Rowland offer that, depending on the context, executive styles varying from highly leader-centric to highly inclusive may end up proving most effective.

Assessment Mechanisms Available in the Private Sector

Since there's no commitment to any one leadership model—in fact, there's a commitment to the idea that we shouldn't even look for one—it's not surprising that so little research has examined which leadership teaching model is best. Ironically, the view that the criteria of good management are necessarily situational may itself reflect the individualistic, competitive nature of corporate culture, which, as mentioned before, tends to prize personal effort and unique genius over collective work and wisdom.

Still, even if we buy into the assumption that every company and every CEO is unique and incomparable, businesses can and do measure themselves against their competitors or earlier performance. And private enterprises can also assess the success of their executive education in comparison to those used by other corporations. At the most basic level, as we'll see in the following chapter about the public sector, surveys of course participants, their supervisors, and the employees they direct can illuminate the strengths and weaknesses of the facilitative approach to teaching and practicing leadership skills in a business context.

But the private sector also has the enviable built-in instruments to measure success and failure that the public sector totally lacks. Although imperfectly quantifiable, businesses can and frequently do survey customers to capture their reactions to managerial intervention. They can ask how clearly a sales representative presented a product, how courteously sales staff handled requests, and how fairly executives resolved consumer complaints. Corporations can also follow their reviews in trade publications and on websites. In addition, private enterprises can track actual sales activity in a way that's not available to public servants: Customers vote with their wallets by choosing one store or company over another, but citizens must resolve their law enforcement problems at their own precinct. Of course, some public sector professionals, such as public defenders, social services workers, or local, state, or national agency employees operate across much larger areas. But there, too, limited "customer"—really, citizen—choice protects them from the rigors of competition, and also deprives them of that source of feedback.

Thus even without any formal quantitative studies, private sector organizations could judge the success of facilitative education in leadership skills. It stands to reason that the nearly universal theoretical support for facilitative training of leaders within the business world would be confirmed by any of these quantitative and qualitative measures available to it.

WHAT THE PRIVATE SECTOR SHOULD LEARN FROM THE PUBLIC SECTOR

Given the lack of investigation into the value of facilitative teaching of leadership in the private sector, we have to refer to programs in the public sector as our benchmark. The advantages that public service personnel and organizations derived from interactive group leadership training promise a similar result in the business world, as long as facilitators acknowledge, accommodate, and utilize the particular characteristics of private-enterprise organizational culture. The specific qualities of corporate culture—and even of different corporate cultures—influence individual and institutional motivations for leadership training, and should shape the leadership development education you offer them.

And just as you, the skilled facilitator, bend your techniques to motivate your particular participants, researchers can use the benchmarks uniquely available to the private sector to learn about a business's health and needs. Compensating for their lack of data on the effectiveness of facilitative leadership training, businesses have other powerful ways to measure it. Surveys of leadership candidates, supervisors and employees, customer questionnaires, and sales tracking provide excellent on-the-ground indications of a company's managerial success compared to other companies or to its earlier performance. Any and all of these instruments might, and should, be used to shed light on businesses' executive advancement approaches and to tailor your most effective facilitative training of private sector leaders.

REFLECTION AND NEXT STEPS

1. **Think back to the previous chapter's Reflection.** Compare your list of the reasons business leadership trainees might resist facilitative training with the reasons discussed in this chapter. Which were the same? Which were different? Would you now add the reasons discussed in this chapter to your list? Why or why not?

2. **Think back again to the previous chapter's Reflection.** What methods or qualities of facilitative training do you now think would best overcome resistance in business organizations?

3. **Reflect on experiences you've had of an organization's resistance to change.** How did it resemble resistance to facilitative instruction? Was it resolved, or not? If it was resolved, how did that happen—through the leadership or not? If it stayed unresolved, in what ways did the leadership err?

4. **Consider what leaders in those businesses might learn from what you now know about facilitative training.** How would you get this across to participants in your classes?

REFERENCES AND RESOURCES

ASTD Research. (2013). *State of the Industry*, Alexandria, VA: ASTD Press.

Avolio, B., B. Bass, and D. Jung. (1999). "Re-Examining the Components of Transformational and Transactional Leadership Using the Multifactor Leadership Questionnaire." *Journal of Occupational and Organisational Psychology* (UK), 72(4): 441-463.

Axelsson, R. (1998). "Towards an Evidence Based Health Care Management." *International Journal of Health Planning and Management*, 13(4): 307-317.

Barker, L. (2000). "Effective Leadership Within Hospice and Specialist Palliative Care Units." *Journal of Management in Medicine*, 14(5/6): 291-309.

Bass, B., and B. Avolio. (1996). *Postscripts: Recent Developments for Improving Organisational Effectiveness*. London: Sage.

Bennis, W. (1999). "The End of Leadership: Exemplary Leadership is Impossible Without Full Inclusion, Initiatives and Co-Operation of Followers." *Organisational Dynamics*, 28(10): 71-80.

Collingwood, H. (December, 2001). "Personal Histories." *Harvard Business Review*: 27-38.

Collins, J. (January-February, 2001). "Level 5 Leadership. The Triumph of Humility and Fierce Resolve." *Harvard Business Review*: 67-76.

Dulewicz, V., and M. Higgs. (2005). "Assessing Leadership Styles and Organizational Context." *Journal of Managerial Psychology*, 20(2): 105-123.

Fiedler, F. (1964). "A Contingency Model of Leadership Effectiveness." In Berkowicz, L. (editor), *Advances in Experimental and Social Psychology*. New York: Academic Press.

Flanagan, H., and P. Spurgeon. (1996). *Public Sector Managerial Effectiveness: Theory and Practice in the National Health Service.* Buckingham: Open University Press.

Garavan, T., and D. McGuire. (2001). "Competencies and Workplace Learning: Some Reflections on the Rhetoric and the Reality." *Journal of Workplace Learning,* 13(4): 144-163.

Goffee, R., and G. Jones. (September-October, 2000). "Why Should Anyone Be Led By You?" *Harvard Business Review:* 63-70.

Hales, C. (1986). "What Do Managers Do? A critical review of the evidence." *Journal of Management Studies,* 23(1): 88-115.

Heifetz, R., and M. Linsky. (2002). *Leadership on the Line: Staying Alive Through the Dangers of Leading.* Boston: Harvard Business School Press.

Hersey, P., and K. Blanchard. (1993). *Management of Organisational Behaviour: Utilising Human Resources.* Englewood Cliffs, NJ: Prentice-Hall.

Hersey, P., and K. Blanchard. (1969). "Life Cycle Theory of Leadership." *Training and Development Journal,* 23(5): 26-34.

Higgs, M. (2003). "Developments in Leadership Thinking." *Leadership and Organization Development Journal,* 24(5): 273-284.

Higgs, M., and V. Dulewicz. (2002). *Making Sense of Emotional Intelligence,* 2nd edition. Windsor: NFER-Nelson.

Higgs, M., and D. Rowland. (2005). "All Changes Great and Small: Exploring Approaches to Change and Its Leadership." *Change Management Journal,* 5(2): 121-151. doi:10.1080/14697010500082902, http://eprints.soton.ac.uk/51416/ (accessed July 23, 2013).

Higgs, M., and D. Rowland. (2001). "Developing Change Leaders: Assessing the Impact of a Development Programme." *Change Management Journal,* 2(1).

Hogan, R., and R. Kaiser. (June 2005). "What We Know About Leadership." *Review of General Psychology,* 9(2):169-180. doi: 10.1037/1089-2680.9.2.169.

Hogan, R., and J. Hogan. (2001). "Assessing Leadership: A View From the Dark Side." *International Journal of Selection and Development,* 9(1/2): 40-51.

House, R., and R. Aditya. (1997). "The Social Scientific Study of Leadership: Quo Vadis?" *Journal of Management,* 23(3): 409-465.

Jaworski, J. (2001). *Synchronicity.* New York: Berrett-Koehler.

Jenkins, D. (2013). "Exploring Instructional and Assessment Strategy Use, Learning Goals, and Educator Demographics in Collegiate Leadership Studies." *Unpublished Preliminary Survey*. Office of Research Integrity and Outreach of the University of Southern Maine. eIRB ID Number 13-01-131

Jenkins, D. (Winter, 2012). "Exploring Signature Pedagogies in Undergraduate Leadership Education." *Journal of Leadership Education*, 11(1): 1-27.

Johnstone, M., and M. Fern. (Fall 2010). "Case-in-Point: An Experiential Methodology for Leadership Education." *The Journal of Kansas Civic Leadership Development*, 2(2): 98-117.

Kegan, R., and L. Lahey. (2009). *Immunity to Change: How to Overcome it and Unlock Potential in Yourself and Your Organization*. Boston: Harvard Business Review Press.

Kets De Vries, M., and E. Florent-Treacy. (2002). "Global Leadership From A to Z: Creating High Commitment Organisations." *Organisation Dynamics*: 295-309.

Kim, H., and G. Yukl. (1995). "Relationships of Managerial Effectiveness and Advancement to Self-Reported and Subordinate-Reported Leadership Behaviors From the Multiple-Linkage Model." *Leadership Quarterly*, 6(3): 361-377.

Kouznes, J., and B. Posner. (1998). *Encouraging the Heart*. San Francisco: Jossey-Bass.

Parks, S.D. (2005). *Leadership Can be Taught: A Bold Approach for a Complex World*, 1st edition. Boston: Harvard Business Review Press.

Senge, P. (1997). "Communities of Leaders and Learners." *Harvard Business Review*, 75(5): 30-31.

Senge, R., A. Kleiner, C. Roberts, R. Ross, G. Roth, and B. Smith. (2000). *The Dance of Change*. New York: Nicholas Brealey.

Singh, A., and N. Muncherji. (February, 2007). "Team Effectiveness and Its Measurement: A Framework." *Global Business Review*, 8(1): 119-133.

Thompson, J., R. Stuart, and P. Lindsay. (1996). "The Competence of Top Team Members: A Framework for Successful Performance." *Journal of Managerial Psychology*, 11(3): 48-67.

Wheatley, M. (2000). *Turning to One Another*. San Francisco: Berret-Koehler.

Yi, J. (2005). "Effective Ways to Foster Learning." *Performance Improvement*, 44(1): 34-38.

Chapter 5

Facilitative Training in the Public Sector

This chapter will cover:

- surprising success with highly resistant participants
- police trainees' and commanding officers' assessments of facilitative leadership instruction
- respondents' comments on facilitation strengths and weaknesses
- how the private sector can apply these results.

FACILITATION SUCCEEDS WHERE YOU'D LEAST EXPECT IT TO

Most leadership instructors agree that adults master executive skills effectively through the participant-directed, collaborative approach of facilitation. They've seen firsthand what a wealth of anecdotal analyses and educational theories suggests: Mature learners hone communication, conflict-resolution, and problem-solving talents best through an interactive group format. But without hard evidence, even experienced facilitators might doubt its appropriateness for, say, a roomful of seasoned cops. We can guess why they might hesitate, since the organizational culture of law enforcement famously includes a respect for authority and for emotional toughness that makes many officers vehemently resist learner-centered, reflective techniques as irrelevant navel-gazing. But if leadership instructors dismiss these public servants as poor candidates for facilitative training, they're ignoring both the power of this approach to transform participants and the willingness of law enforcement personnel to undertake their own transformation.

My experience and research has taught me that, despite plenty of initial discomfort with participant-driven settings, criminal justice learners do in fact develop outstanding executive abilities when given maximum control of their courses under minimal guidance of a facilitator. Law enforcement participant and supervisor feedback on interactive leadership training shows that facilitators who are sensitive to the specific personal and institutional pressures on their participants can anticipate and employ the challenging characteristics of their professional culture to kindle personal and organizational growth. In fact, cumulative, longitudinal, and multi-population statistical surveys show that facilitative training for leaders in law enforcement effectively achieved departmental aims of improving officers' communication, mediation, and cooperative skills. Perhaps more significant, they appear to have transformed trainees' thinking and feelings not only in professional, but in personal contexts as well. And if it worked for this difficult population, tracking its successes and analyzing its limitations offers very valuable lessons for facilitators in the business world, too.

AIMS AND STRUCTURE OF THE PUBLIC SECTOR LEADERSHIP PROGRAMS

The programs surveyed here, a bachelor of arts and a master of arts in organizational leadership (BOL and MOL) at Woodbury University, demonstrate the difficulties and benefits of facilitative training for public-sector personnel (mostly sworn officers and professional staff of the Los Angeles Sheriff's and Police departments). A primary content goal was to strengthen their Community-Oriented Policing (COP) leadership skills. A primary structural goal was to design intensive programs to accommodate adult learners' work and family stresses. (For example, graduation requirements were flexed for, and thus successfully met by, two delivering mothers!) More unusual, the programs had to relate to the unique demands on police force members: hazardous assignments and the need to mediate volatile, sometimes violent, community relations.

Following adult learning theory, the curriculum focused on both the personal and professional interests of law enforcement personnel. After courses in communication skills, private- and public-sector organizational management, diversity issues, and contemporary community affairs, a final "capstone" project required participants to write a comprehensive paper applying everything they had learned in the program to their private and public lives. All enrollees had to articulate their motivations for pursuing the degree, assess the gains they made toward those goals, and link leadership theory with their own practice of leadership in the classroom—a culminating assignment that would provoke valuable reflection in business leadership trainees as well.

In keeping with the adult learning paradigm, the programs also ensured a participant-driven agenda through participants' continuous evaluations of course format and content. For example, at the close of each course learners gave their views not only on class length and workload but on its applicability to work and to their personal and professional aims—another excellent practice easily transferrable to leadership development in the private sector.

RESEARCH DESIGN

Cumulative, longitudinal, and multi-population confidential surveys that I created for police leadership candidates and their supervising officers yielded statistical data about the effectiveness of facilitative training. As noted, consistent with the participatory nature of facilitation, at the last session of each undergraduate or graduate leadership program from 2002 to 2009, participants judged its format and relevance, as well as their own professional and personal development. Responses of 44 BOL course takers and 117 MOL candidates to a nearly identical survey were each combined to produce cumulative BOL data and MOL data. In 2010, an online follow-up survey was administered to program alumni (92 alumni out of 135 solicited, or 84 percent of the six undergraduate cohorts' alumni and 95 percent of the 11 graduate cohorts' alumni answered); and their responses were also merged to provide cumulative data. Another survey (through the Los Angeles Sheriff's Department Professional Development Unit) received responses from 30 supervising officers of BOL and MOL alumni (out of 84 solicited). So we can investigate the value of interactive group leadership training in the public sector cumulatively, by considering eight years of end-of-class participant surveys; longitudinally, by examining end-of-class and follow-up alumni surveys; and through multi-population queries, by studying the responses from BOL and MOL enrollees, alumni of both programs, and Los Angeles Sheriff's Department alumni's supervisors. Some questions in each instrument required yes-or-no answers; some offered a range of responses; and several invited open comment. Because those remarks greatly enhance the quantitative data, I've included representative samples of them.

BOL PARTICIPANT SURVEY RESPONSES
Course Mechanics

Beginning with neutral queries on the course, last-class surveys revealed that 81.8 percent of class members approved of courses' length, while a small minority (2.3 to 11.4 percent) found them somewhat brief, somewhat long, or decidedly too long. Similarly, 84.1 percent of respondents rated the workload appropriate, while 2.3 percent evaluated it as overly light and another 13.6 percent described it as at least somewhat too demanding.

What Business Leadership Educators Can Learn

Although not everyone liked the length and workload of the courses, most participants found them manageable, despite their intensity and fast pace. This result indicates that highly motivated full-time employees are willing to work hard in a program that feels relevant to their work and personal lives.

Professional Relevance

Next, the survey posed more nuanced questions about the professional relevance of the bachelor's in organizational leadership. A full 95.5 percent agreed that, as a direct result of the program, they are better able to handle conflict at work (with 61.4 percent strongly agreeing and 34.1 percent agreeing), while 4.5 percent remained noncommittal about their improvement. Also, 97.7 percent of respondents thought they had become more effective employees (with 65.9 percent concurring strongly, 31.8 percent concurring, and 2.3 percent neutral). In addition, 77.3 percent of respondents reported having started new policies and plans at work using information and ideas learned in class. In fact, more than two thirds (68.1 percent) found program information very relevant to law enforcement work, and less than a third found it only somewhat applicable: 54.5 percent stated that they used course material almost daily, 13.6 percent reported applying it at least weekly, and 31.8 percent stated that they employ the information occasionally.

Other questions probed perceived advances in work-related skills. The survey showed that 97.7 percent of BOL candidates felt their critical thinking had improved, 91 percent experienced a heightened capacity for creative problem-solving, and 95.5 percent believed that they better understood their own decision-making process. In particular, they attributed greater competence in writing (93.2 percent) and in speaking (88.6 percent) to BOL activities.

What Business Leadership Educators Can Learn

Interestingly, respondents appeared to value broad communication skills and increased reflectiveness in their thinking at least as much as the substantive content they learned. Business leadership trainees would likely appreciate the chance to gain in communication, mediation, decision-making, and cognitive abilities, in addition to technical knowledge.

Emotional Intelligence

What's especially interesting, though, is that almost all respondents felt that not just their technical but also their interpersonal and internal psychological skills—what's called "emotional intelligence"—had deepened. Fully 95.4 percent saw in themselves increased cultural awareness and sensitivity to diversity issues, and 83.7 percent reported a greater capacity to respond to community needs. More unexpectedly, 95.4 percent of survey-takers agreed or strongly agreed with the statement that completing the program made them better able to manage their personal lives. These results match participants' stated motivations for pursuing the degree program: 36 percent undertook it primarily to get a promotion; 27.3 percent hoped for a promotion, transfer, or better job; and 13.6 percent expected a better job only. Twelve class members (roughly 27 percent) who received promotions or transfers while in the program mentioned advancement as a central aim. But remarkably in line with adult learning theory, more than 90 percent of participants reported a combination of incentives for enrollment, including personal growth and increased professional leadership skills in criminal justice and social service fields.

What Business Leadership Educators Can Learn

The previous chapter noted differences in motivations for leadership education between public servants and businesspeople, specifically that public-sector employees may feel less concern about job security. But it's crucial for business-sector facilitators to gauge what proportion of personal versus corporate reasons their participants enter leadership development. Even if business trainees enroll more for professional concerns, it's likely that the experience of facilitative education will prove equally transformational for them as for public sector trainees, so facilitators should prepare them—and themselves—for that unexpected benefit.

MOL PARTICIPANT SURVEY RESPONSES
Course Format, Professional Relevance, and Emotional Intelligence

Much like the BOL candidates, most MOL enrollees expressed satisfaction with the program's basic format of course length and workload: 87.9 percent approved the length of the courses, 11.2 percent found them somewhat brief and 0.9 percent judged them as far too brief; and 72.2 percent of candidates termed the workload appropriate, with 1.7 percent evaluating it as somewhat light, 25.2 percent describing it as somewhat demanding, and 0.9 percent judging it overly demanding.

Assessments of the program's contribution to their professionalism also resembled those of BOL enrollees: 95.5 percent of MOL respondents believed that, as a direct result of their program, they were better able to handle conflict at work (with 53.4 percent strongly agreeing and 43.1 percent agreeing), while 1.7 percent were neutral and another 1.7 percent disagreed. A majority claimed to have become more effective employees (with 51.3 percent strongly assenting and 45.2 percent assenting). Finally, 79.1 percent stated that they had initiated new policies and plans at work that were derived from what they had learned in class.

Even more than those in the BOL, the MOL respondents thought that the program sharpened both general and specific professional skills. For 99.1 percent, critical thinking appeared to have been enhanced; 95.7 percent noticed strengthened creative problem-solving; and 94.8 percent asserted that they could more clearly analyze the way they made decisions. Regarding specific abilities, 93.2 percent saw betterment in their writing and 92.2 percent felt their public speaking had improved through the program.

Again like their BOL counterparts, most MOL participants credited their program with developing interpersonal abilities, with 90.6 percent reporting increased cultural awareness and sensitivity to diversity issues and 77.8 percent reporting greater responsiveness to community needs. More notably (and again like BOL respondents), 90.5 percent agreed or strongly agreed that they had become better at managing their private lives. Thirty-two respondents (roughly 27 percent) mentioned promotions and transfers received while in the program as one element of their motivation for enrolling but, like most BOL candidates, the majority of MOL respondents cited personal as well as professional goals. One participant detailed this blend of personal and professional growth: "The program helped me look at situations in my home and at work in a more comprehensive way, not just from the cynical cop point of view; it has made me a better professional."

What Business Leadership Educators Can Learn

Significantly, enrollees in the master's program reported improvement in basic skills to similar degrees as those cited by the bachelor's candidates, but found greater improvement in thinking and interpersonal abilities as compared to the undergraduates. This result confirms two claims about facilitative training: It's especially well-suited for sophisticated learners (as graduate students are more schooled, and on average older, than undergraduates), and it exercises intellect and emotions in addition to teaching course material. So business leadership instructors may use it with confidence to advance the capacities of participants at every level, and they should also expect deep transformations in the reasoning and attitudes of midlevel to higher-level trainees.

ALUMNI SURVEY RESPONSES AND WHAT BUSINESS LEADERSHIP EDUCATORS CAN LEARN
Demographics

Of the 92 alumni who completed the follow-up survey, 63 percent were male and 37 percent female, with an average age of 44. Twenty-six percent had graduated college and 3 percent had done post-graduate work, with 68.5 percent having already earned a master's degree. Within the Los Angeles Sheriff's Department, 11 held the rank of deputy (with officers, the lowest rank), nine were sergeants, 10 were lieutenants (midlevel ranks, although some categories of lieutenant rank higher), one was a captain, two were commanders, one was a chief (the highest rank), and 22 were professional staff (ranging from lower-level operations and administrative assistants to higher-level supervisors and administrators). In addition, there were seven officers, six sergeants, three lieutenants, two captains, one deputy chief, and professional staffers from the Los Angeles and neighboring police departments.

What Business Leadership Educators Can Learn

These demographic data substantiate the impression that most people who pursue leadership training—whether for academic credit, work requirements, or personal growth—are non-traditional mature learners with increasingly elevated levels of college education. In fact, most who were already in leadership positions (lieutenants and higher) had already earned a master's degree. Among the non-ranked professional staff, whose positions would correspond to those of supervisors and administrators in the business sector, many were continuing their higher education. The takeaway: Your leadership training must appeal to well-educated, sophisticated middle and upper levels of management and supervisors.

Uniqueness of Facilitation

Responses suggest that alumni of both undergraduate and graduate facilitative programs recognized them as quite distinctive from others in objectives and design. Specifically, they found that these courses contrasted markedly with college classes they had taken in terms of subject matter (62.2 percent), teaching style (74.2 percent), and participants' role in class (66 percent). Even more, they felt that the program courses differed from standard peace officer training courses in terms of subject matter (76.3 percent), teaching style (76.3 percent), and participants' role in class (76.9 percent). Still, 87 percent of respondents did not find it difficult to get used to the BOL or MOL class format (intensive four-hour classes once weekly for seven [BOL] or five [MOL] weeks), although 13 percent did find it somewhat difficult.

Many alumni ascribed the uniqueness of the programs to the format itself, citing its supportiveness, intellectual creativity, interactive teaching and classwork, snappy pace, and collaboration with a cohort of working professionals. Comments noted that these accelerated programs did a good job of accommodating the professional and family pressures on persons long out of school, but did not seem "dumbed down" as did other peace officer training courses they had taken to satisfy departmental promotion requirements.

What Business Leadership Educators Can Learn

Law enforcement work requires endless classes in new weapons, police technology, administration, and street-smart sociology. If trainees in this profession report that the facilitation differs radically from their many previous courses by virtue of its intellectual and emotional demands and benefits, they mean what they say. Business leadership facilitators can be sure that in the business community as well, few trainees will have experienced such support, cooperativeness, intensity, and ingenuity in their earlier education, and should keep in mind how novel—for better or worse—interactive learning can seem at first.

Format and Professional Relevance

As a result of the program format and applicability, many alumni reported having felt "much more involved than in other courses," and appreciated that "people's opinions were never deemed wrong, but you were forced to . . . have some backing for your view." They specified that general class participation kept course activities interesting. One respondent confessed to having felt "relieved to complete the program" but found later that he "missed the high quality of instruction and personal style of teaching."

Most respondents also underscored the program's relevance, traced to classes' drawing on participants' "real life experiences and expertise" and exercising actual work skills. One field region operation-patrol deputy identified the program's demands to "stand and speak in front of our peers" as a skill he needed "on a daily basis." Another alumnus valued the MOL program because "it showed me the different approaches to leadership and the 'How?' of being a leader," thereby filling a leadership training gap for line supervisors below the rank of captain.

Generally, alumni found course concepts high-level, multi-dimensional, and pragmatic: "We learned to consider different 'lenses' with which to evaluate different situations. We also learned to construct strategies for implementation and to expect, and manage, resistance and conflict." As one MOL graduate put it, the "inviting and informal" program encouraged expression, valued diversity, and was "not a one-size-fits-all approach." Further outcomes included "being able to communicate well with anyone at work" and learning to do "not only the minimum, but to think out of the box and to do your best." Still, many found the quantitative analysis (statistics) unit in the MOL difficult and, in the judgment of some, irrelevant, and one alumnus expressed disappointment that the expensive "required books were not used to their fullest."

What Business Leadership Educators Can Learn

Open comments from alumni on questions about program format and professional relevance vividly illustrate their appreciation of the program's pointed focus on work. As established by adult learning studies, professional relevance comprises one of the most powerful draws for adult attention and learning. Clearly, facilitative leadership developers in the private sector can and should be equally vigilant in designing the format of their courses to capture trainees' interest in workplace tasks and to practice workplace skills.

Effects in the Workplace, Explained

Consequent to completing the programs, 60 percent of alumni thought their degree helped them earn a desired promotion or transfer and 76 percent believed the program boosted their self-confidence and gained them the respect of fellow officers. While self-esteem and assessing others' good opinion are clearly subjective judgments, the survey could measure those internal views: Around 70 percent thought the program strengthened their own confidence in their leadership, acceptance of new ideas, communication of new ideas, comprehension of other viewpoints, their ability to resolve disputes and solve problems, skill at setting and achieving group goals, and ability to work with the community they served.

Surprisingly, even respondents who were not promoted or who did not instigate changes in their departments stated that they would still encourage others to enroll in the programs for personal growth, and to break away from the limited definition of "success" as climbing the ladder. In fact, 89.5 percent of BOL and all MOL respondents had referred at least one person to the programs.

Open comments explained these effects as stemming from greater facility for connecting with others and for analyzing problems "from a leadership perspective." Many respondents cited specific techniques and ideas learned in the BOL and MOL facilitative programs that they used in their work: First was conflict resolution, followed closely by group dynamics, communication and listening skills, problem-solving, mediation, and ethical reasoning. In the words of one, "I credit the program with becoming a better communicator . . . [which increased] my self-esteem . . . and allowed me to challenge myself." Another reported that "the program impacted my life in many ways. I am a stronger communicator and able to stand up for the ethics I believe in. I saw myself mature as a leader, developing stronger teamwork and understanding the diffi-culties and stages all of us must go through to accept changes in the workplace."

While any leadership instructor would lecture on much the same content, respondents found that actively experiencing material in participant-driven peer groups made the lessons stick: "I learned to collaborate and display leader-ship while working in groups [by] exchanging ideas in a positive and supportive environment." Increased confidence in decision-making; better responses to ethical problems; innovative problem-solving strategies; heightened awareness of institutional politics, culture, and values; developing teamwork and dele-gating tasks; time management; and dealing with personnel—alums felt all these capacities had been polished by practice. In particular, graduates recog-nized that seeing and learning to tolerate various leadership styles gave them the emotional intelligence to "approach a problem with confidence . . . and flexibility: If you can connect with peers and subordinates in a common language, anything is possible."

Specifically, most respondents recognized the paradoxical benefit of learner-driven groups in teaching them how to recognize and combat group-think. They also learned to "think globally and utilize the strengths of each individual." By coming to know each other individually, most found that they shared a vision despite cultural diversity, disagreement, or resistance to inno-vation. One alum pinpointed a prime lesson: "The area that I use the most is getting people that work under and alongside me to make changes and work through the transition. I stick to the four-quadrant formula we learned of intro-ducing the change and telling the benefits, listening to the defensiveness but not accepting it, praising employees when I see small efforts of implementation of the new change . . . and giving ownership of the successes to the employees."

What Business Leadership Educators Can Learn

Squarely in line with adult learning theory, these programs captured trainees' attention and maintained accessibility by proving maximally relevant to their professional lives. The high degree to which participants immediately applied new learned material and sharpened skills in the workplace increased their worth. For leadership developers in the private sector, direct relevance to work-place tasks and needed abilities will make your course similarly valuable.

But the particular takeaway is the success of facilitative methods in making leadership learning stick. The interactive, hands-on, repeated practice of group negotiation, cooperative planning and execution, and public presentation seemed especially able to polish executive skills and to raise trainees' confidence through a concretely experienced improvement in work-related capacities.

Comfort and Discomfort

To gauge a more sensitive issue—alums' psychological comfort with the interactive, participant-driven nature of facilitative leadership training—respondents were asked, somewhat sneakily, whether they thought any other participants seemed uncomfortable with course activities. They estimated that 80.7 percent of colleagues had enjoyed the BOL or MOL class activities and that 19.3 percent had somewhat disliked them. Seventy-one percent of alumni guessed that other classmates had not felt at all uncomfortable during the classes, 27 percent felt others had seemed somewhat uncomfortable, and another 2.2 percent observed that some class members had been very uncomfortable. Fifty-eight percent opined that other participants had not wanted to avoid class activities, but 36.7 percent thought others had somewhat wanted to avoid them and 2 percent thought others had definitely wanted to avoid them. Still, 99 percent of respondents stated that other participants seemed to get more comfortable with class activities over time.

Another indirectly posed question aimed to plumb alumni reactions to the facilitative structure by asking which BOL or MOL activities they had found irrelevant. An overwhelming majority (90.9 percent to 96.6 percent) of alumni surveyed identified its core teaching techniques (working in groups, having participants decide course goals, not getting the answers from instructors, having to resolve participants' varying opinions, and having to talk about inner feelings) as not irrelevant.

At this point, graduates were asked directly whether they themselves had found program activities challenging—a line of questioning that elicited more equal splits, which are shown in detail in Table 5.1.

Table 5.1. Have You Found Program Activities Challenging?

Activity	Yes (%)	No (%)
Working in groups	55.6	44.4
Having participants decide course goals	37.5	62.8
Not getting the answers from instructors	23.9	76.1
Having to resolve participants' various opinions	45.5	54.3
Having to talk about inner feelings	36.4	63.6

In written comments, some alumni testified to their personal difficulty talking in front of a group. Yet most found these individual challenges necessary, as one remarked, to "improve ourselves and our department" by becoming "much better prepared to lead a group. I understand some of their thinking, concerns, wants, and needs."

Finally, respondents were asked point-blank whether any BOL or MOL activities had been uncomfortable for them, yielding evidence of the psychological vulnerability many criminal justice learners felt in the facilitative environment, as shown in Table 5.2.

Table 5.2. Have You Found Program Activities Uncomfortable?

Activity	Yes (%)	No (%)
Working in groups	15.9	84.1
Having participants decide course goals	8	92
Not getting the answers from instructors	11.6	88.4
Having to resolve participants' various opinions	18	82
Having to talk about inner feelings	23.5	76.5

Most significant, open comments demonstrated that, despite some personal difficulty with these tasks, the majority of alumni saw them as crucial for law enforcement officers who, as a respondent noted, "protect the public, enforce the laws, and lead others in times of unrest. We have to work with others, the public and co-workers in the classroom, on the street, and in the office." The bulk of the comments acknowledged the value of these challenges, sometimes bluntly: "I paid you money to teach me. Not cuddle me. You came through and taught me about group dynamics and real leadership. It was a little confusing, but the dividend was far greater. Thank you."

What Business Leadership Educators Can Learn

Facilitators teaching business leadership can learn much from these questions on participant comfort levels. Since these programs were populated by learners more than usually resistant to self-direction and emotional expression, their eventual acceptance of those demands especially strongly confirms the wide applicability of facilitation. As shown in the previous chapter, relatively greater job insecurity and the traditional corporate valuation of competitiveness may make business leadership candidates resist different aspects of facilitation more than public employees; for example, trainees from private enterprise may resist this approach's enforced cooperation and group accountability. But acknowledgment of such resistance, and creativity in applying characteristics of corporate culture to interactive, communal leadership learning, can be as successful as the public-sector programs investigated in this chapter.

Collegiality and Conflict

Respondents identified some problems with their BOL or MOL colleagues, shown in as shown in Table 5.3.

Table 5.3. Problems With BOL or MOL Colleagues

	Yes (%)	No (%)
Some participants seem to think they know more than their peers.	36.2	64.8
Some participants seem to think they know more than their supervisors.	32.9	67.4
Some participants are too relaxed at work.	17.4	82.6
Some participants are too relaxed in the community.	13.1	86.9

Numerous survey-takers noted that not every group member pulled his or her own weight or showed respect for instructors and colleagues. A respondent complained that "one student can make a bad decision on a project and cause everyone's grade to suffer. There are leaders, followers, and group dynamics. That was a very important issue that I learned." Some voiced resentment of "honors students" having gotten high scores on group projects with less effort than others put in, and a number vented their irritation with "self-centered and inconsiderate" classmates. One alum cautioned that talking openly about one's feelings "could prove to be offensive," while another complained about "cliquish behavior" and one instance of plagiarism. While most mentioned the unexpected depth of discussions, one respondent highlighted "the level of resistance from older and non-law enforcement students to grappling with the issues."

A good number suggested that before enrolling, everyone should fully commit to the depth and "the very fast pace of this accelerated program. Adult learning works very well if all students work hard and participate . . .. I went to [this program] because . . . other schools only want you to write paper after paper and there is no real quality interaction and no real criticism." A few argued that all participants should already have taken basic English, speech, and business classes. Interestingly, one respondent stated alums should meet again in "follow-up sessions every year or two to compare notes and reassess."

Here alumni comments reveal particular weaknesses of the facilitative format: Some participants contribute less to group projects than others, and a few try to monopolize discussions, others don't seem to understand the material. Nevertheless, a vast majority of respondents strongly favored the cohort-centered teaching model and requested that the university organize "the most professionally diverse cohorts possible—our cohort was ideal because the students came from diverse professional backgrounds (private sector, engineering, law enforcement, education, health, and so on)."

What Business Leadership Educators Can Learn

The value respondents found in the diversity of the trainee cohort attests to both an adult learning advantage (mature learners bring richly varied experiences to the classroom) and an adult learning disadvantage (mature learners bring the whole range of capacities to the classroom). As a facilitator in the business sector you will need to exploit the first (that's the fun part) and manage the second with differentiated education (to review, see Part I, chapter 2)—that's the creative challenge.

Group Identity and Leadership

Alumni widely appeared to believe that the programs altered classmates' and their own internal attitudes and outward behaviors toward others in the group. Most respondents (67.4 percent) claimed their program made them feel part of a team (including 31.5 percent who felt only somewhat so). By the end of the program, 82.6 percent felt very connected and 17.4 percent felt somewhat connected to other participants. Seventy-seven percent of respondents felt much more personally confident by the end of the program, while 22 percent felt somewhat more so.

The majority (64.8 percent) thought that they had witnessed a lot of good leadership, while 34.1 percent judged that they had witnessed some. Perhaps more telling, 71 percent of respondents believed that they themselves had practiced very good leadership in the programs and 29 percent reflected that they had practiced fairly good leadership. In particular, one respondent observed that, once united, the cohort actually "had more 'power' than the instructors . . . to determine class content."

What Business Leadership Educators Can Learn

Classic corporate culture, as noted, tends to reward competition and individual genius more than group efforts. But the business world is changing, even in bastions of capitalism, and is becoming more appreciative of the power of communal creativity and the expanded resourcefulness gained by collective work. So the ability to provide facilitative (that is, cooperative, interactive, and supportive) training of future private sector leaders is on the cutting edge of this wave—ironically making this cooperative teaching technique the most competitive out there!

Teachers and Topics

Some suggestions touched on teachers and topics. Several urged that only the "strongest instructors" should teach: "If you are in a nontraditional setting, it is good to have some of your professors to be doctors." Early topic ideas (incorporated in later courses) were to broaden the curriculum to cover private-sector as well as public-sector organizations, and to discuss race relations, favoritism, and discrimination in the workplace. But one alumnus just wanted more structure in the learning environments, saying, "I'm not the classic 'adult learner' type."

What Business Leadership Educators Can Learn

Respondents' reactions underscore the increasing educational levels and sophistication of leadership trainees uncovered in the demographic questions. But I think that whether you personally possess degrees higher than those of your trainees weighs less in their esteem than your own grasp of the material and comfort with facilitative techniques of conveying it. Still, it's noteworthy that leadership development has become a scholarly field in its own right, which elevates the respect in which your participants, and you, should hold it.

SUPERVISOR SURVEY RESPONSES AND WHAT BUSINESS LEADERSHIP EDUCATORS CAN LEARN

Demographics

Thirty Los Angeles Sheriff's Department supervisors of sworn alumni responded to the survey sent through the department's professional development unit. They were asked to assess the facilitative programs in leadership, based both on what they knew or had heard about them and on their observations of BOL or MOL graduates under their command. Eighty percent of respondents were male and 20 percent were female. Of these, 20 percent had had some college, 36.7 percent were college graduates, 33.3 percent had master's degrees (MA, MS, pastoral degree, or counseling license), and 3.3 percent held a doctoral degree. The respondent group consisted of six sergeants, nine lieutenants, six captains, four commanders, two chiefs, one assistant sheriff, and two holding other titles.

What Business Leadership Educators Can Learn

By comparing these demographic results with those of alumni we see that over twice as many participants as their superior officers held post-graduate degrees. This confirms the impression that leadership candidates are increasingly highly credentialed. It stands to reason that such a trend would be found in business circuits as well. Thus leadership developers in the business realm can expect, and should plan for, a growing proportion of well-schooled, sophisticated trainees in their courses.

Uniqueness, Value, and Relevance

A modest majority of supervisors (45 percent BOL to 57.9 percent MOL) perceived that both BOL and MOL courses differed from those of other college classes because of their facilitative format. A heftier majority (57.9 percent to 68.4 percent) felt these leadership programs differed from other peace officer training courses in both material and facilitative format. But supervisor comments most clearly demonstrated their view of the uniqueness of the BOL and MOL, which they ascribed to "the high level of class participation"; "the curriculum being leadership-based and tailored for the law enforcement professional"; and "the facilitative nature of classes, with the opportunity for students to facilitate subject-specific dialogue and discussions."

All supervisors stated that they found it not at all difficult to justify department support for the BOL and MOL programs. Only one had heard complaints from participants in either program, and only a very small minority (0.0 percent to 11.1 percent) believed that participants found it irrelevant to work in groups, decide course goals themselves, forgo getting the answers from instructors, resolve participants' varying opinions, or talk about feelings.

What Business Leadership Educators Can Learn

One of the more surprising results of this study is that nearly all senior leaders—commanding officers of enrollees and alumni of the BOL and MOL programs—recognized the unique characteristics of facilitative leadership training, and valued those as job-appropriate. As noted in the previous chapter, corporate management may have quite different motivations for encouraging leadership development. But if they're like the overwhelming majority of these public service supervisors, they will also acknowledge the specific merit and relevance of the facilitative education of future leaders.

Comfort and Discomfort

A slightly larger minority of supervisors (0 percent to 42.9 percent) believed that those same activities were challenging for participants—interestingly, more than the participants themselves did! And a still larger number of supervisors (7.1 percent to 53.3 percent) felt that those same activities specific to the programs' facilitative format may have made participants uncomfortable.

What Business Leadership Educators Can Learn

As a facilitator in the world of enterprise, you can take heart from these results, which indicate that supervisors assumed a greater level of discomfort among trainees than the trainees themselves reported. The reason for this discrepancy may be that supervisors lacked the benefit of actually experiencing the initially difficult activities and the talents of an able facilitator to help trainees recognize, express, and overcome their discomfort. That gift is one that you are entirely able to offer trainees in your business leadership courses as well.

Teamwork and Leadership

Based on what supervisors knew or heard about the programs, most felt that participants worked very much like a team (85 percent) and became very comfortable with the class activities over time (84.2 percent). Over 63 percent thought the participants learned about good leadership in the BOL and MOL programs. Sixty percent of the supervisors believed that the participants had themselves practiced a lot of good leadership in the BOL and MOL, while 30 percent thought participants practiced good leadership somewhat and 10 percent thought they did so not at all.

Seventy percent of the supervisors had supported participants' requests for promotions or transfers; of these, slightly fewer than half (42 percent) ascribed the promotions primarily to candidates' successful completion of a program, while 58 percent ascribed them mostly to other factors. Seventy-five percent of supervisors noted an improvement in leadership skills on the part of BOL and MOL participants.

In trainees' work with fellow officers and in the community, the near majority to majority of supervisors (47.4 percent to 65.0 percent) thought that the BOL and MOL helped participants feel more confident in their leadership abilities, develop or accept new ideas, communicate their own ideas, understand other points of view, resolve disputes, solve problems, and set and achieve group goals.

Other supervisors responded that the program helped their supervisee establish a mentoring role with others, "engaging more with others in developing resolutions to work-related matters and . . . defusing conflicts," as well as showing greater "ability to identify and utilize staff's weaknesses and strengths [and] . . . when necessary to be an effective manager versus an effective leader."

When asked about any negative attitudinal consequences of the programs, based on what they had seen or heard, supervisors displayed largely positive responses, with only a very small minority (0 percent to 10.5 percent) finding that participants seemed to think they knew more than their peers, seemed to think they knew more than their supervisors, or act too relaxed at work or in the community. One supervisor recalled that a participant had expressed frustration at not being able to use the tools he had learned. Yet most supervisors had witnessed graduates' current application of leadership techniques and concepts practiced in the programs, specifically "conflict resolution," "working with groups," "dealing with difficult employees," "more comprehensive plans," and "innovative ideas."

What Business Leadership Educators Can Learn

The fact that seasoned supervisors witnessed improved leadership in their personnel—many of whom they did not even know were pursuing a leadership program—should encourage all educators in executive skills. It's also a surprisingly strong recommendation for the facilitative approach to leadership education, since it's far more likely that enrollees and alumni who've invested lots of time and effort in a course would claim its value than would supervisors, whose role includes critiquing those they command. Similarly, in the realm of enterprise, although no quantitative evidence yet exists, it's likely that effective facilitative leadership development will be recognized as readily by top-level executives as it will be by course graduates.

Surprising the Supervisors

Supervisory respondents were surprised by some effects of the programs. One mentioned "the ability to perceive globally how excited they were to obtain their instructional goals in such a short amount of time with the flexibility of the program; they were proud of themselves and how it related to the workplace."

They also offered specific suggestions to strengthen the BOL and MOL programs, including "more financial assistance" and making sure "that supervisors know that a subordinate is enrolled in the program." They overwhelmingly supported the program, believing, in the words of one, that it "broadens our vision and helps us to be diversified leaders."

What Business Leadership Educators Can Learn

If the supervising officers felt surprise at the enthusiasm, efficacy, and applicability of the BOL and MOL programs, so did the researcher! Of course I had hoped for favorable assessments and thoughtful, constructive critiques, but I have to admit I mostly felt real surprise by the unanimity and warmth of support the commanders gave. Although, as we know, very little hard research has been conducted on facilitative (or any) leadership education in the private sector, I think the results of this public-sector study suggest that business trainees, and their supervisors, will be similarly surprised at the value of facilitative training of leaders in the world of enterprise.

RECOMMENDATIONS FOR THE PRIVATE SECTOR

Adult learning theory asserts that mature learners gain the most from training that's tailored in content and format to their motivations and capacities. To provide such teaching we should take our lead from ongoing participant evaluations. So the first recommendation emerging from this study is that facilitators should continuously survey participant opinion and, as much as possible, incorporate the curriculum and structural changes participants propose. For example, although the current case transpired within the public sector, the facilitator integrated a whole unit on private-sector organizations into the curriculum which trainees had requested as highly relevant to their work.

Interestingly, though, almost all of respondents' suggestions concerned structural issues that pertain equally to business and service settings. According to the evaluations:

- Courses should be taught by the most qualified instructors, preferably with degrees as high as those the participants are earning.
- Instructors should not be over-generous in assessment, but should score each participant for his or her contribution rather than on the efforts of his or her group.
- Before starting a course, participants should know and agree to the level of commitment it requires.
- Participants entering programs should have roughly equivalent mastery of writing and speaking.

In sum, the cumulative, longitudinal, and multi-population statistical data presented here strongly suggest that law enforcement officers increase their executive abilities through learner-driven, interactive group facilitation—provided the instructor can explore and manage any resistance stemming from their organizational culture. As one alum astutely observed, "almost every one of (my colleagues) felt they learned more in this class . . . but were reluctant to credit the facilitator style with the learning outcome because of the lack of comfort with . . . the departure from the traditional." Facilitative leadership trainers in the business world should recall that, while corporate organizational culture differs from civic organizational culture, it will also generate resistance, albeit for quite varying reasons: Where law enforcement officers may initially resist self-direction, debate, and introspection, trainees in private enterprise may at first dig their heels in against self-sacrifice for the group, communal creation, and genuine camaraderie. In both private and public sectors, then, you as the facilitator have the responsibility of helping your trainees break their mental and attitudinal habits so they can grow into the best leaders they can be.

By tracking the limits and achievements of the interactive training of leaders in the public sector through multiple surveys of participants and supervisors, I could measure its efficacy more accurately than through anecdotes or theorizing. We know that executive talent—in any organizational context—takes more than substantive knowledge. It requires diplomacy, respect for others, clear communication, ethical responsibility, and self-knowledge. Apparently, the facilitative learning environment in which participants actively and repeatedly practiced these qualities supported the transformation of public-sector learners into leaders. And as we saw in the previous chapter, the learner-driven qualities that make facilitative leadership training successful in the public sector also allow it to transfer, through your sensitive adjustments, to executive arts training in the private sector.

SUMMARY

Feedback from participants and alumni underscored certain areas of concern about facilitative training in the public sector. While some pointedly requested instructors with advanced degrees (doctorates), most complaints centered on the varying abilities—intellectual and emotional—and educational levels of fellow learners, particularly those at the master's level. Although classes knew that differentiated instruction is a valuable tool in facilitation, the majority of participants had assumed colleagues would have better writing and verbal skills—an expectation that was often disappointed. Additionally, some suggested that facilitators should be less generous to "social loafers" who did not partici-pate as much as harder-working group members but got the same group grades.

As a whole, current participants and alumni viewed the facilitative course format and activities as effective in, and relevant to, law enforcement leadership training. They were generally comfortable with programs' length and work-load. Most important, candidates and graduates of both programs largely felt that the experiential techniques they had repeatedly practiced in class—even if with considerable initial reluctance and discomfort—let them better apply those skills at work, especially conflict resolution and an increased sensitivity to diversity issues.

Respondents and their supervisors recognized the programs as unique, differentiated from other college or police training by the encouraging atmo-sphere, intellectual rigor, and group relationships. But maybe what's most striking in the cumulative and follow-up surveys is that the majority of recent and past participants felt that the facilitative approach to learning leadership made them better able to manage challenges in their personal as well as in their professional lives.

REFLECTION AND NEXT STEPS

1. **What surprised you in this chapter?**

2. **Weigh the importance of the organizational culture**. Since their respect for rank and emotional toughness makes law enforcement officers very resistant to participant-driven, cooperative education, what qualities of the leadership programs assessed in this chapter seemed most useful in overcoming their resistance?

3. **Recall the previous chapter.** List some reasons private sector trainees—say, midlevel business managers—might resist facilitative training. Now drawing from the current chapter, what qualities of a leadership training program might best overcome business candidates' resistance?

PART III

BRASS TACKS HANDBOOK

Chapter 6

Best Practices and Resources

This chapter will cover:

- the facilitator guide to projects and games that go beyond same-old "discussion" to teach leadership interactively

- sample scripts and game pieces for classroom activities

- how to grade groups and individuals

- film and print resources, plus guidelines for using them

- participant comments and reactions showing the transformative power of these activities and materials.

FACILITATOR GUIDE

Learner-centered teaching maximizes participants' emotional and intellectual involvement. These activities help you build a group culture that engages learners, respects them, and directs their leadership qualities toward a common aim.

We've seen that a random assortment of individuals needs a brief period of reliance on a leader to mature into a unified, empowered whole. So definitely give directives at the start to ease participants from passive to active habits of learning and working. Throughout the course, initiate each session with a short presentation of material that participants can then apply in individual or group exercises, and finish each session with a wrap-up activity to sum up what they've learned. Here are some pointers on your all-important communications.

Communication Tips

- Speak as little as possible! Three points per verbal communication and five per page are sufficient. But make your voice carry throughout the room.

- Be a performer (but not the star). Vary the tone of your voice, body language, and rate of speech to reinforce content and show your enthusiasm.

- Repeat questions and key points throughout your presentations. Use different words and modalities—verbal, visual, and kinesthetic (such as mini-charades).

- Let participants set the pace of learning. Their body language and faces will clue you in if you're going too fast or too slow.

- At the beginning of each session or unit, frame questions to check listeners' familiarity with the topic so you can gauge their interest and adjust your depth of detail. Remember that the participants— not you—determine success, so aim to deliver what they want to hear, how they want to hear it.

- Remember that trainees pick up everything. If you're uncomfortable with your subject, they'll know; if you aren't feeling well, they'll know. Acknowledge your humanity.

- Help the group resolve any unfinished business. Ask questions like, "At the end of last session, we were talking about some pretty interesting [or controversial or frustrating] aspects of [fill in the topic]. Do you want to go back and explore those further?"

- Understand that the buck stops with you. If something goes wrong, take the heat without blaming others, discuss the problem calmly, and use it as a teachable moment.

- Keep in mind that most organizations and classes run top-down, and remember how novel, and maybe threatening, facilitation can seem. Your first job is to show that interactive learning and leadership is effective, meaningful, and fun.

Group Process Troubleshooting

We've seen from Creighton that every interaction involves both content and process—the stated task and the unstated context of leadership, conflict, and cooperation. Most of the time, we disregard process, even though it's the main source of individual and group problems. But facilitators can't ignore group dynamics if they want to prevent or deal with those concerns and model good management. Proactive facilitators stay on the lookout for them. To do so, they consistently monitor class members' participation levels and membership—the sense of belonging to the group—as well as issues of influence, communication, decision-making process, work dynamics, atmosphere, and norms. (Part I, chapter 3 provides a useful worksheet to help you track classroom dynamics.)

Assessing Individuals in a Group Context

At the very start of the course, when you collaborate with participants to set assessment criteria (you might look ahead to chapter 7), you'll clarify that interactions with the group will weigh in individuals' evaluations. But expect to see some role rigidity, a common problem that usually stems from our habitually favoring one aspect of ourselves (brainiac, peacemaker, class clown) or, more rarely, from deep-seated defense mechanisms. Bringing role rigidity to the class's attention—tactfully and without embarrassing anyone—lets participants "try on" different roles and gives the whole group an instructive and corrective interpersonal experience. Inviting greater role flexibility encourages people to stop typecasting themselves and others, keeps the class lively, and lets you assess individuals more easily.

To evaluate individuals, then, you'll draw upon your observations of group dynamics to measure each participant's collaborative efforts. So in addition to grading members' personal projects, appraise them in terms of group-centered criteria:

- engagement in group work and discussions
- helping the group stay on task and on time
- appropriate management of time
- cooperation
- effort to bring group to consensus
- use of varied work and problem-solving methods
- crediting others for their ideas
- appropriateness of feedback and comments
- responsiveness to feedback and comments
- capacity to listen
- clarity of comments
- value of ideas contributed to the group
- exercise of leadership.

CLASSROOM ACTIVITIES AND PROJECTS

To increase trainees' self-awareness and to make sure your instruction is differentiated so it's equally accessible to visual, aural, and kinetic learners (see Part I, chapter 2 and Part III, chapter 7), ask everyone to take a learning styles inventory (see the Learning Style Quiz activity later in this chapter) early in the course. It will help you and the participants design activities and projects capitalizing on their different learning preferences. The following tried-and-true best practices engage participants by creating experiences in accord with their learning strengths and interests—the essence of facilitation. In addition to these, innumerable variations can be found (see the Resources section at the end of this chapter; in an academic setting, online material is usually free if you acknowledge the copyright and reference the link). Under every activity listed you'll find its **purpose**, any special **preparations** you'll need to do, a scripted **directive** you'll tell the class, and **follow-up** discussion questions.

First-Session Interviews

Purpose

This alternative to the standard first-session demand to "introduce yourself to the class" highlights the team-building aspect of facilitation. Slightly nontraditional questions encourage, but do not force, in-depth sharing, and the dyad (pair) structure begins forming connections that feel safe between colleagues.

Instructions for the Facilitator

Ask participants to pair up—ideally with someone they've never met. If there is an odd number of participants, you will be someone's partner. Spread out animal cards (small pictures of animals) face-up on the floor, using more than the number of class members so everyone gets a choice. Give each dyad two handouts with the following interview prompts:

- Can you tell me two unusual things that happened in your lifetime?
- Do you have any special talents or hobbies?
- What person do you most admire? Why?
- What color best describes who you are and how you feel?
- Pick an animal from these cards. Can you tell me why you selected that animal?
- If you were that animal, what would you say?

Directives to the Class

"Using this list of questions and these cards, interview your partner for three minutes and then switch. Each person will introduce his or her partner to the class. Try to give the class the best possible idea of your partner. You may take notes, and I'll tell you when it's been two and a half minutes." (At two and a half minutes, say "In 30 seconds, please switch.")

Follow-Up

This fun (and often funny) activity signals the personal nature of the course and gives everybody a first acquaintance (even if someone's was you!). Participant comments illustrate the surprising depth of feeling this introductory exercise can access. One marveled, "I saw all the animal cards on the floor and my mind just took off in different directions trying to guess what the cards were about. It was interesting to see the puzzled faces on the rest of the class. Funny how something that simple can throw a group of people into a guessing spin." Another recounted, "Upon entering the classroom the first thing I noticed was the new person sitting who . . . introduced herself as our professor. I instantly felt a level of ease and comfort in her unassuming role as our instructor, leader, and confidante. The floor was filled with cards that had a variety of animals pictured on them; as I sat, I looked for the animal I would choose, a jaguar. I choose the jaguar because it is sexy, graceful, confident, powerful, beautiful, and ferocious, and when asked what would I say, I stated, 'Watch my swag,' which translated to, 'observe me in motion and witness my magnificence.'"

Debriefing

Purpose

Posing these questions after every project or activity fulfills two goals: It helps participants process their experience, and it gives you feedback on the project or activity.

Instructions for the Facilitator

To spark discussion, invite comments: "Let's talk about what doing this was like for you," and ask the following questions. Or, you may ask participants to answer them briefly on paper:

- Was the task completed?
- What was learned?

- What was it like to work with your group/the class? Did people work as a team?

- How would you assess others' roles in this task?

- Did group interactions seem fair, or did one or more persons take over?

- How would you assess your role in this task?

- Did you complete the task but ignore how people felt, or whether everyone participated?

- Did you focus more on having people enjoy working together than on the task?

- What might have gone better in the group/class?

- Did this experience seem similar or different to working in your organization? How?

Diversity Bingo

Purpose

Another popular organizational behavior activity, this game sensitizes participants to invisible diversity issues and to the effects of prejudice.

Instructions for the Facilitator

Give each participant a Diversity Bingo worksheet (which you can find on the next page). You may alter these to highlight specific diversity issues (see the Resources section at the end of the chapter).

Directives to the Class

"We are playing Diversity Bingo. To win, you will need to circulate in the room and get people to sign off in the squares whose descriptions apply to them. But each person may sign your Diversity Bingo card only once, even if that person fits the description in more than one square."

Follow-Up

In addition to the debriefing questions ask:

- Did you notice assumptions being made about yourself? About others?
- Which squares were the easiest to fill? Why?
- Which squares were hardest to fill? Why?

Diversity Bingo

Obtain the signatures of people who match the description in the squares.

A person who. . .

knows what haggis tastes like.	was not born in a hospital.	speaks two languages fluently.	has foreign-born grandparents.	celebrates Cinco de Mayo.
has attended three rock concerts.	paints or draws for relaxation.	recycles regularly.	has immigrated to the U.S.	is left-handed.
knows sign language.	married someone with a different religion.	has gone through Greek rush.	ate in an ethnic restaurant within the last 24 hours.	knows what granita is.
knows what Yom Kippur is.	has experienced being stereotyped.	usually has his/her name mispro-nounced.	knows what an upside-down pink triangle symbolizes.	has an *abuela*.
owns a dog or a cat.	lives near a shopping mall.	attends religious services weekly.	follows football closely.	plays computer games to relax.

Learning Style Quiz

Purpose

Participants will increase their understanding of their own learning style, and also become aware of different types of intelligence.

Instructions for the Facilitator

Look over a few of the websites that offer a free, immediately scored Learning Style Quiz or Inventory (see the Resources at the end of the chapter). Recommend the best two.

Directives to the Class

"Pair up, or make a group of three, and meet out of class to take a Learning Style Quiz together. Figure on 15 minutes for the quiz and five or 10 minutes to talk about your reactions to the experience. Plan on using your own computers or taking turns on one. Two good sites are [the sites you chose]. Jot down some notes because we'll all discuss this together at our next session."

Follow-Up

At the following session, do a debriefing of the quiz experience. Survey whether anyone disagreed with the quiz findings (some will) and why (some may have reasonable objections but some just dislike being "categorized" or "diagnosed.") Also survey who felt the quiz explained something they never understood about themselves, and how that feels (many will feel relieved that their way of auditory, visual, verbal, or kinesthetic knowing is an accepted mode of intelligence; many will have a better grasp of why they like or dislike particular tasks). Include the topic of different types of intelligences in the discussion, and ask the group to summarize all the types of learners they've now heard about. Encourage members to take their, and others', particular learning styles into account as they design projects in the course.

Hobby Shop

Purpose

Polishes public speaking skills and encourages taking a limited risk of self-disclosure.

Instructions for the Facilitator

Participants share something of themselves by teaching the class about a hobby or interest of theirs.

Directives to the Class

"I want each of you to teach the class about a hobby or interest you have—for instance, cake decorating, calligraphy, candle- or incense-making, building a doll collection, installing a swimming pool, cooking, playing a musical instrument, or snowboarding. Whenever possible, your presentations should include a demonstration of related equipment and a hands-on activity your classmates can do."

Follow-Up

Participants may ask any questions, but the facilitator will focus on the process: how presenters chose what to share, their feelings about bringing this part of their lives to the room, and how they saw its reception by colleagues.

Dinner Party

Purpose

This fun activity stimulates thinking about leadership exemplars, and shows individuals' values and creativity without risking too much self-disclosure at an early point in group development.

Instructions for the Facilitator

Figuring one table per group of three participants (one group may have four if necessary), set up small tables with tablecloths (or a reasonable facsimile) and other simple "dining table" props (such as small centerpiece candles, artificial flowers, glassware, or napkins). If it's impossible to get tables, push desks together and cover with a tablecloth, or at least group chairs around "centerpieces" on a tablecloth on the floor. Give each group a poster-sized sheet of paper or cardboard and some markers.

Directives to the Class

"As you can plainly see, each group is hosting a dinner party in this very elegant restaurant, The Leaders' Inn! You have five minutes for each member to decide which living, historical, or even imaginary person exemplifying leadership you would like to invite. Each member will explain to the other members why he or she has chosen that guest. Then, each group will thoughtfully orchestrate seating arrangements for all guests and members. Finally, each group will design a menu, and write its guest list and menu on the poster board. When we are all done, each group will present its dinner party guest list and reasons for it, seating arrangements, and menu to the entire class for discussion. Make your own group decision as to who will present what aspect of your dinner party to the class—guests and reasons, seating arrangements, and menu."

Follow-Up

Figure on 10 minutes to debrief as a full class. Put the names and menus up to see similarities. Past classes have invited Jesus, Oprah, people's moms and future children, Hitler, and Viktor Frankl to our "tables" in this open-ended activity, which also provided a great common experience for the class to refer back to later. At the end, you may vote on which group had the best guest list and reasons, seating arrangements, and menu. It's also fun to provide an extra "dessert" by bringing chocolates for everyone in the class!

Tower Building

Purpose

Especially useful for kinetic, "hands-on" learners, this widely used organizational behavior exercise has been modified endlessly: Teachers have used cupcakes, ice cream sundae fixings, toothpicks and gumdrops, clay and Popsicle sticks, and myriad other materials with which participants construct a tower, dog house, bridge, or nearly any free-standing edifice meeting certain height and strength requirements. The task trains participants to cooperate in groups and to manage the pressures of material and time limitations (or, at least, rewards them for doing so). Each group picks an observer to record how well the group followed directions and interacted.

Instructions for the Facilitator

Before class: Whatever building materials you choose, you must have them fully prepared for each group. You may wish to use a stopwatch to add to the excitement. (For more ideas, see the Resources section at the end of this chapter.)
In class: Divide the class into groups large enough to appoint one person as its observer. Distribute materials.

Directives to the Class

"Using only the materials provided, your group will attempt to build the highest free-standing and unattached [name the item] that can withstand being blown by me for five seconds. Every group must first elect an observer, who will do nothing but note how well the group follows directions. Here are your directions: You have 10 minutes to plan, during which time you may not touch any of the materials; eight minutes to build; and 12 minutes to debrief your process.

I will give you a two-minute warning before you must begin to build and a two-minute warning before you must finish. Begin now." (Give two-minute warnings naming the next step, and when time is up, say "Now start [fill in the step].")

Follow-Up

Have the observers share what they saw, and use the debriefing questions to explore group dynamics that helped or hindered.

One, Two, All

Purpose

This exercise strengthens reflection, communication, and cooperation skills.

Instructions for the Facilitator

Think of a topic that class members have discussed but do not need to research.

Directives to the Class

"We've discussed [name the topic], but don't yet know what each of you thinks about it. Find a partner, and every pair will have two minutes to reflect quietly on the topic, then another two minutes to discuss it together. Then each pair will present their thoughts to the class." (Give 30-second warnings; call times to move to next step.)

Follow-Up

After all dyads have presented, use the debriefing questions to invite a general discussion about the process and results of this activity.

Company Town

Purpose

Variously named, but most commonly known as "Blue/Green Enterprises," this standard organizational behavior game can be accessed through numerous websites and publications, which provide instructions and scorecards (see the Resources section at the end of the chapter). In this "Prisoner's Dilemma" activity, participants are instructed to work "for the good of the whole company," but usually ditch cooperation to compete and win as the "department" to which they've been assigned.

Instructions for the Facilitator

Divide participants into groups and give each group envelopes with four blue and four green index cards (or different-colored poker chips or other game pieces), along with a tally sheet.

Directives to the Class

Hand each group a sheet printed with this sole directive: "You are a member of a small work unit within a division of the company. Your unit's task is to exchange resources in the form of blue and green pieces with another work unit in another division of the company. The objective is the accumulation of net positive points in a series of eight exchanges. However, because of the company's "need to know" policy, there can be no communication verbally or non-verbally between the units of the company. Your goal is to obtain the most net points for all groups, since you all work in different departments but for the same company." Give no additional directives! If needed, assure them they will figure it out on their own.

Follow-Up

Use the debriefing questions to analyze successes, failures, and, especially, the group processes occurring during this game. Most groups will focus on irrelevancies such as the number of cards/chips/game pieces they have; the possible plans of other groups; or how they can send messages without using words. Some people abdicate leadership to others, claiming they are too confused; and some are truly afraid of being seen as a competitor or as a collaborator.

You're on Your Own

Purpose

The objective of this activity is to have groups figure out and finish a task without instructions or speaking. Usually, they quickly realize that they must make a design with their pieces, but many will assume, wrongly, that they need pieces from other groups. This assignment underscores the value of considering alternative solutions to problems.

Instructions for the Facilitator

Before class:

- Copy one sheet of Observer Directives (on the following page) for each group.
- Take one square sheet of construction paper per group of four or five participants, and add one more sheet for yourself.
- Stack the sheets together and cut them into five irregular pieces (that is, make a jigsaw puzzle).
- Fill one envelope per group, plus one for you, with all pieces of the square puzzle.

In class:

- Divide the class into groups of four or five. Give each group an envelope. Keep one.

- Pick one person from each group to act as a participant observer. Take each aside, and silently give each a copy of the Observer Directives sheet.

Directives to the Class

Give the class no directions; if needed, assure them they will figure it out on their own.

Follow-Up

In past sessions, groups have created arrows, Stars of David, houses, and other objects. The most successful group included a kindergarten teacher and finished the square in one minute! After the activity, debrief the participant observers on what they saw. In addition to the debriefing questions, ask all class members:

- What was it like to be given a task with no direction?
- What was it like to be given a task without being allowed to talk or ask questions?
- Who initiated the task? Did everyone participate? Did everyone participate equally?

Observer Directives

- Who is willing to give away his/her pieces?
- Is every group member involved in trying to solve the problem?
- Is there a group member who will not share his/her piece(s)?
- Who initiates trying to solve the task?
- Note laughter and if groups want to interact with each other.
- What did your group do when it completed the task? Withdraw? Laugh at the other groups? Try to help or to interfere with the other groups?

Two-Minute Paper

Purpose

This activity solicits ongoing written feedback about course content.

Instructions for the Facilitator

To use as an icebreaker in the beginning of class, ask participants what they already know about the topic, what they want to learn, and obstacles to their learning it. Or, you may use it as a wrap-up to measure understanding of course concepts.

Directives to the Class

"I'm giving you two minutes to write the shortest paper in academic history. Tell me what you know or think about [the topic]."

Follow-Up

Learners may read their papers to the class and open the floor to questions, or you may solicit comments from all on the topic and on the process of expressing their thoughts.

Movie Night

Purpose

Movies or film clips provide concrete models of leadership behavior or its absence. Especially useful for people who are not comfortable as readers, use these clips to spark general discussion and debate.

Instructions for the Facilitator

After consulting the list of published sources (see the resources at the end of the chapter), choose the film or clip that illustrates an area of leadership that the class has struggled with.

Directives to the Class

"Please ponder these issues as you watch the movie." Then read or hand out the following topics:

- recognizing leadership characteristics and behaviors
- identifying follower behaviors
- applying leadership theories learned in class to characters
- identifying decision-making by characters and its effects
- evaluating different managerial styles.

Follow-Up

Discussion topics will depend on the film as well as viewer reactions. Many leadership-movie guides exist (published or online), and sometimes list specific issues and questions. The resources at the end of the chapter present time-proven works and, for each, identify themes and questions that, with the debriefing questions, generate lively debate.

Leadership Photo Collage

Purpose

This activity challenges trainees to capture the essence of leadership visually. It's especially good for visual thinkers and those who feel uncomfortable writing or speaking, so it helps you provide differentiated instruction (see Part I, chapter 2).

Instructions for the Facilitator

Everyone needs a digital camera for a day or so.

Directives to the Class

"I want you to create a photographic collage showing the essence of leadership that you will present to the class. You may go anywhere and take as many photos as you wish, but your final collage can have no more than 10 photographs. Prepare a PowerPoint presentation. You may add music to enhance your presentation."

Follow-Up

Participants usually share digital cameras, which encourages cooperation. Most enjoy adding music to their presentations. (Be sure to use the debriefing questions.)

Projective Drawing

Purpose

This classic art therapy activity helps participants understand the different roles they play in various groups.

Instructions for the Facilitator

Distribute two pieces of paper and coloring supplies such as markers or colored pencils to each participant.

Directives to the Class

"On one sheet of paper, draw yourself at a typical dinner at home with your family. On the second sheet of paper, draw yourself at a typical meeting at work."

Follow-Up

After participants are finished drawing, have them, one at a time, show their work to the group and describe their scenes. Classmates can ask questions and note differences and similarities of the pictures, but remind them that this is not about artistic talent and there should be no judgments. In addition to asking the debriefing questions, suggest that viewers:

- Note colors used in the scenes.
- Compare people's sizes and positions, and the amount of detail in each picture.

- Decide which drawing would be more appealing to be part of.

Paging Dr. Freud

Purpose

Group members study, write about, and present to the class their findings concerning a specific organization or informal group of their choice. The exercise hones observation and analytical skills, and conveys what they have learned about group dynamics.

Instructions for the Facilitator

Suitable groups include the Hell's Angels, a book club, the city council, an exercise class, a choir or band, a local softball team, AA meetings, workplace gatherings, and their own classroom interactions.

Directives to the Class

"Pick any group you can observe, observe it in operation, and present your findings about its interactive dynamics."

Follow-Up

Compare the dynamics evidenced in the presented groups. Apply the same analytical categories used to assess class groups to the groups studied. (Use the debriefing questions.)

Detectives

Purpose

Learners become authorities on specific aspects of a subject, all of which are linked, so the activity encourages collaborative learning, listening, and organizing skills.

Instructions for the Facilitator

Calculate how many small groups of equal number (one may have an extra learner if necessary) you will have. For each group, take one piece of construction paper and write on it the same number of facts about one specific topic as there are members in that group. Cut the pieces of paper so that each part of it carries one fact and all parts will fit together to re-create the whole sheet of paper. Each group's sheet should have facts on a different topic.

Directives to the Class

"Everyone will research the one fact he or she has on his or her piece of paper and present it to the group. Then the group will decide how each member's specific information fits into the topic as a whole. Finally, each group will present its topic to the class."

Follow-Up

Use the debriefing questions to open a discussion on the organizing process each group carried out.

Graduation Party Planning

Purpose

This long-term planning project, which may last through each semester of a multi-year program, provides hands-on practice in two important leadership skills: creating a vision statement and making group decisions.

Instructions for the Facilitator

Within your budget, space, and other restrictions, offer the class a culminating party, every detail of which they must plan.

Directives to the Class

"I'm inviting you to your own graduation party, but you will need to decide on every single aspect of it, and complete every task involved, as a group—food, place, music, décor, dress code, guest policy, and theme. Have fun, but you are responsible for considering and resolving every single logistical issue needed to make it happen."

Follow-Up

Mature learners often roll their eyes when they are told to plan their graduation party two years in advance, feeling it's irrelevant or too simple. But after brainstorming about possible venues, menus, guest policies, themes, music, dress code, and decorations, participants realize they will have to overcome a whole series of obstacles to realize their plan. Commonly, this process transforms the task from simply throwing a party to envisioning where they will be two years down the road. At different points in this long-term project, pose debriefing questions.

Course Evaluations

Purpose

A central element of facilitative teaching, requesting feedback helps participants process their experiences and fine-tune their definitions of success. Additionally, incorporating such feedback into the curriculum improves the course for the future.

Instructions for the Facilitator

Review the class members' evaluations discussed earlier (Part II, chapter 1 and in the Appendix). Hand out evaluation forms in the last or next-to-last session.

Directives to the Class

"Please fill out these forms, which will help me know more about your experience in this course. These are absolutely confidential, and your feedback is very valued."

Follow-Up

As noted, tracking a series of end-of-class evaluations longitudinally lets you provide the best possible facilitative training in leadership. This activity is the ultimate debriefing; by this time participants should be skilled analysts of their personal and group processes.

RESOURCES AND HOW TO USE THEM
Books and Articles
Guides and Books for Movies

Coupe, K., and M. Sansolo. (2010). *The Big Picture: Essential Business Lessons From the Movies*. St. Johnsbury, VT: Raphel Marketing.

Dallaire, R. (2004). *Shake Hands With the Devil: The Failure of Humanity in Rwanda*. Cambridge, MA: Da Capo Press.

DiSibio, R. (2006). *Reel Lessons in Leadership*. Aiken, SC: Paladin Group.

Krakauer, J. (1999). *Into Thin Air: A Personal Account of the Mt. Everest Disaster*. New York: Knopf Doubleday.

Lansing, A. (1999). *Endurance: Shackleton's Incredible Voyage*, 2nd edition. New York: Basic Books.

Phillips, D. (1993). *Lincoln on Leadership: Executive Strategies for Tough Times*. New York: Warner Books.

Thiagarajan, S., and G. Parker. (1999). *Teamwork and Teamplay*. San Francisco: Jossey-Bass.

Guides to Leadership Training Activities

Fletcher, A. (2002). *FireStarter Youth Power Curriculum: Participant Guidebook*. Olympia, WA: Freechild Project.

Muller, H.J., and P.A. Parham. (1998). "Integrating Workforce Diversity Into the Business School Curriculum: An Experiment." *Journal of Management Education*, 22(2): 122-148.

Pfeiffer, J.W., and J.E. Jones. (editors). (1972). *Annual Handbook for Group Facilitators*. Iowa City: University Associates.

Websites for Leadership Training Activities

Diversity Bingo Ideas

Culbertson, H. (2013). "Cultural Diversity Bingo," http://home.snu.edu/~hculbert/bingo .htm (accessed July 24, 2013).

"Diversity Bingo." http://www2.mercer.edu/NR/rdonlyres/27732149-E7FB-4A17-9704 -8A76A28B7877/0/DiversityBingo.pdf (accessed July 24, 2013).

SUNY Cortland. (2013). "Cultural Diversity Bingo." http://www2.cortland.edu/offices /advisement-and-transition/cor-101/goals-objectives/diversity.dot (accessed July 24, 2013).

Tower Building Ideas

"Free Child Project." www.freechild.org/Firestarter/towerbuilder.htm (accessed July 24, 2013).

"On Course Newsletter." www.oncourseworkshop.com/Awareness003.htm (accessed July 24, 2013).

"TeamPedia Tools for Teams." www.teampedia.net/wiki/index.php?title=Building_the _Tower (accessed July 24, 2013).

Other Activities and Projects

"Air War College Center for Strategic Leadership Studies." http://leadership.au.af.mil /sls-tool.htm (accessed July 24, 2013).

Badenhorst, M. (2013). "Staff Training and Professional Development." http://staff -training.wikispaces.com (accessed July 24, 2013).

"Team Building Portal Activities, Games and Articles," Business Balls.com www.team buildingportal.com/ (accessed July 24, 2013).

Fleming, N.D. (1992). "Learning Styles Inventory." www.vark-learn.com/english/index .asp (accessed July 24, 2013).

Fleming, N.D., and C. Mills. (1992). "Not Another Inventory, Rather a Catalyst for Reflection." To Improve the Academy: Paper 246. http://digitalcommons.unl.edu /podimproveacad/246 (accessed July 25, 2013).

Icebreakers.ws, www.icebreakers.ws/ (accessed July 24, 2013).

Insight Media. www.insight-media.com/ (accessed July 24, 2013).

Internet Resources for Leadership-Themed Movies

CASAA (Canadian Association of Student Activity Advisors)

http://leadershipteacher.webnode.com/other-resources/movies-and-videos-for-leader ship-class/ (accessed July 24, 2013).

"Hartwick Leadership Classic Literature & Film Cases." www.hartwickinstitute.org/hhmi _faq.htm (accessed July 24, 2013).

"Kantola Productions,." www.kantola.com (accessed July 24, 2013).

"Leadership Teacher." www.fireleadership.gov/toolbox/lead_in_cinema_library/lead_in _ cinema.htm (accessed July 24, 2013).

North Georgia College and State University. www.northgeorgia.edu/Leadershi p/Default_1col.aspx?id=1562 (accessed July 24, 2013).

Leadership-Themed Movies and Movie Clips

Apollo 13 (140 min): Based on the real-life crisis on board the spacecraft on April 13, 1970, the movie illustrates the theme, "failure is not an option." An explosion during its lunar mission created problems that could be solved only through teamwork, creative thinking, and complete focus. This movie provides in-depth observation of these skills along with problem-solving, communication, trust, and loyalty.

Billy Budd (94 min): Based on Herman Melville's novel, this film shows that both bad leaders and good ones with false notions of leadership can equally destroy innocence and order.

Bridge on the River Kwai (161 min): This classic war film demonstrates that devotion to a single goal can cause a leader to lose sight of his overall mission.

Catfish (94 min): This documentary considers the connection between technological and interpersonal communication, and explores ethics in the age of the Internet.

Conspiracy (96 min): This movie traces the tragic consequences of a meeting during which Hitler's highest leaders designed the genocide of the Jews. It provides examples of how great leadership talents can be used for evil.

Courage Under Fire (117 min): This film weighs varied leadership behaviors and their effects in real incidents during the Gulf War.

Crash (115 min): This movie considers a multiplicity of cultural, racial, and social tensions in Los Angeles, California, through the interwoven stories of the characters, many of whom work in law enforcement.

Crimson Tide (116 min): During a period of instability in Russia, military units loyal to the ultranationalist Radchenko gain control of a nuclear missile installation, and threaten nuclear war if either the American or the Russian government attempts to confront them. The commander of the United States' nuclear strategic missile submarine USS *Alabama* picks a smart but inexperienced officer to help him in this crisis, and the movie explores the value of different leadership talents.

Dead Poets' Society (128 min): This unusual film attempts to differentiate helpful mentoring and invasive influence on others.

Gandhi (191 min): This movie tracks the life and politico-philosophical development of Mohandas Gandhi, leader of the nonviolent movement that ended Britain's colonial rule of India during the first half of the 20th century.

Gettysburg (254 min): Opening with words spoken over a map of the two armies at Gettysburg, the battle that will decide the outcome of the Civil War, this film lets viewers analyze and compare not only the military, but the political leaders of the North and South.

Glory (117 min): Capt. Robert Gould Shaw, a patrician white officer, trains and leads a company of black Union soldiers, most of them former slaves. The film demonstrates the widespread disrespect and unequal treatment accorded them by the Union that profited from their efforts and deaths. In the film, Captain Shaw comes to understand his own prejudices, to respect his men, and to elevate their own view of themselves.

The Hill (123 min) or *The Last Castle* (remake of *The Hill*) (133 min): Set in a British "glasshouse" (military detention camp), the film examines the dangers of harsh leadership and irresponsibility.

Hoosiers (115 min): This sports film celebrates an Indiana high school basketball team that wins the 1951/1952 state championship despite its small size and low expectations.

Hunt for Red October (134 min): The threatened entry of a Soviet ship into American waters elicited a range of responses.

Looking for Lincoln (120 min): Used in tandem with *Lincoln on Leadership* by Donald Phillips (see Books and Articles), the film shows how Lincoln overcame his personal weaknesses to lead.

Lord of the Flies (1990 remake) (90 min): Shipwrecked on an island, young boys must organize their society in order to survive. Tensions quickly surface as the group divides between two very different leaders.

Master and Commander (138 min): Despite its historical inaccuracy (the British were in fact fighting the United States, not France), the film presents excellent set pieces showing leaders making difficult decisions during extreme hazards.

Miracle (136 min): The U.S. Olympic hockey team demonstrates team-building by finding the right personnel and creating synergy, but also by coaching players according to their individual uniqueness.

Platoon (120 min): Set during the Vietnam War, the film explores the relationships between a gung-ho new recruit and the cynical seasoned soldiers he comes to respect.

Remember the Titans (114 min): This sports movie focuses on changing the culture of a team and a town.

Serpico (first scene clip): Serpico, a new cop, is eating at a diner with his training officer. The training officer does not pay for his meal—a violation of police ethics that forces Serpico to question his training officer's values.

Shackleton's Antarctic Adventure (41 min): Used after reading *Endurance: Shackleton's Incredible Voyage* by Alfred Lansing, the film shows Shackleton's leadership, and rescue, of his crew from some of the harshest conditions on the planet.

Shake Hands With the Devil (113 min): After reading the identically titled book, this very graphic movie about the UN's dismissal of Lt. Gen. Romeo Dallaire's warnings about the 1994 genocide in Rwanda illustrates the frustrations of leadership.

Sister Act (scenes 15 and 16): This film portrays transformational leadership, inclusiveness, and thinking outside the box. Played by Whoopi Goldberg, the main character hides in a convent as part of a witness protection program, runs afoul of the Mother Superior, and is punished with the job of coaching the choir. But she transforms the task and the choir, bringing it cohesion, synergy, and self-esteem through novel assignments and inclusiveness. The choir's newly brilliant performances attract new church members—the church's primary goal.

The Social Network (120 min): The young business leader who founded the social networking website Facebook must deal with the resulting lawsuits.

Sound of Music (174 min): This film is based on the true story of the Von Trapp Family Singers. The scene wherein the children attempt to play ball with their father's then-fiancée, the Baroness, illustrates "in-group" and "out-group" dynamics. The leadership qualities of the Mother Superior and of Captain Von Trapp and Maria as they hide the children from the Nazis, as well as the follower mentality of the oldest daughter's boyfriend, who joins the Nazis, generate lively discussions.

Storm Over Everest (109 min): After participants read Jon Krakauer's *Into Thin Air,* watching this movie vividly demonstrates how the lack of leadership can cause tragedy.

Tora Tora Tora (144 min): This film dramatizes the Japanese attack on Pearl Harbor and re-examines the traditional view of General Short and Admiral Kimmel as leaders.

Twelve Angry Men (96 min): Set in a steamy 1957 New York City jury deliberating room, this film focuses on the art of persuasion and influence. Viewers observe critical thinking and decision-making, and can discuss how each juror justified his conclusion of guilt or innocence—facts, prejudice, past experiences, emotion—and which appear to be leaders.

Twelve O'Clock High (132 min): A tough general turns the lackluster U.S. Army's Eighth Air Force bomber pilot unit into a powerful team in World War II.

Wall Street (126 min): This film depicts the costs of immoral leadership. Encouraged by a corrupt corporate raider, an impatient young stockbroker breaks all the rules, including the law against trading on inside information.

Wizard of Oz (101 min for the current version; original is 112 min): This classic aligns with Tuckman's Stages of Group Development, and it's a great way to show how their training has changed participants' perceptions and illuminated leadership issues they never noticed before.

SUMMARY

Websites and publications with group activities and resources abound. Not all are as thoroughly tested as the ones in this chapter, but by now you have a sense of what works "in the trenches." Look for activities and materials that encourage both individual talents and collective interaction, as they will best strengthen the ideals and the skills of leadership.

REFLECTION AND NEXT STEPS

1. **Imagine you are a participant instead of the instructor.** Which activities in this chapter would you find appealing? Which might be scary or seem silly? As the instructor, do you agree with those assessments? Why or why not?

2. **Consider the activities or projects that might cause conflict or be uncomfortable for learners.** Why might they? How could you make those experiences feel safe without watering them down?

3. **Think of a favorite movie or book.** How does learning about facilitative teaching of leadership make you see it anew? Do you think participants in your course might view their favorite books, films, or shows differently now?

REFERENCES AND RESOURCES

Creighton, T.B. (2005). *Leading From Below the Surface: A Non-Traditional Approach to School Leadership*. Thousand Oaks, CA: Corwin Press.

Garmston, R. (2007). "Collaborative Culture." *Journal of Staff Development*, 28(2): 55-57.

Gregory, R. (April-June 2010). "The Art of Collaborative Leadership: Practices and Disciplines." *International Journal of Educational Leadership Preparation*, 5(2), http://cnx.org/content/m34618/1.2/ (accessed July 25, 2013).

Heifetz, R.A., R.M. Sinder, A. Jones, L. Hodge, and K.A. Rowley. (1989). "Teaching and Assessing Leadership Courses at the John F. Kennedy School of Government." *Journal of Policy Analysis and Management*, 8(3): 536-562.

Jenkins, D. (Winter 2012). "Exploring Signature Pedagogies in Undergraduate Leadership Education." *Journal of Leadership Education,* 11(1).

Johnstone, M., and M. Fern. (Fall 2010). "Case-in-Point: An Experiential Methodology for Leadership Education." *The Journal of Kansas Civic Leadership Development,* 2(2): 98-117.

Johnstone, M., and M. Fern. (May 2008). "Intervention and Leadership: Tactical and Strategic Skills, Can They Be Learned?" Unpublished manuscript, John F. Kennedy School of Executive Education, Harvard University, Cambridge, MA.

Kegan, R., and L. Lahey. (2001). *How the Way We Talk Can Change the Way We Work.* San Francisco: Jossey-Bass.

Parks, S.D. (2005). *Leadership Can be Taught: A Bold Approach for a Complex World,* 1st edition. Boston: Harvard Business Review Press.

Chapter 7

Experiential Lesson Outlines

This chapter will cover:

- a complete guide to course creation for different class venues and lengths
- tips for facilitators, whether novice or expert
- step-by-step outlines for the toughest leadership development lessons, with goals, activities, and assessments.

HOW TO USE THIS CHAPTER

If you've looked through the previous chapter, "Best Practices and Resources," you're ready to create specific design documents. But as the poet Robert Burns reminds us, the best-laid plans of mice and men go oft awry. This guide will help you meet the most common challenges in your quest to make your group of learners cohesive and cooperative. And since experiential education is learning by doing, plus reflecting, this guide not only identifies activities and readings to do, but also the issues you and your participants will weigh as you become an executive team.

First, this chapter gives you basic tips that are worth learning if you're a facilitation newbie and reviewing if you're an expert. The next part will help you analyze the goals and anticipate potential glitches in each of your major teaching hurdles, in the order you'll attack them: changing participants into colleagues, keeping the course facilitative, demonstrating leadership transactions, and helping participants integrate differing views. Then, for each of these core leadership goals, you'll get both general guidelines and three experiential lesson outlines with activities and readings on leadership from this and other books—so you'll also have your immediate teaching objectives. (For details on activity preparation, materials, class instructions, and follow-up discussion, review the previous chapter. If an activity serves more than one purpose, it's mentioned here in more than one place.)

Each lesson outline can be adjusted for longer or shorter class periods and works equally in a full-degree program, training course, or unit in a leadership class. It's crucial to manage session time from the start, so figure on using about 10 percent of your time at the start to convey basic information and instructions, about 60 percent of your time in activities or projects, and 30 percent of your time for questions and discussions after each activity.

You'll note that a full third of your time is earmarked for debriefing following every activity. Even a short Q&A about whatever has just happened in the class serves three crucial purposes: It focuses participants on the central leadership issue of group process; it lets them air negative or positive reactions instead of bottling them up; and it allows you to gauge the success of the activity.

Varying the types of learning modalities keeps people from sitting still too long and letting their brains return to a passive mode. So aim to alternate learning behaviors (research, discussion, presentations, and games) and to insert physical movement and breaks. For example, you might divvy class time into three components, with short intermissions: First block: your short presentation, an activity, and debriefing; next block: group games or projects and a debriefing; last block: group presentations and—you guessed it—a debriefing to generate and process feedback.

A prime way to keep sessions lively is by parceling meetings into short units sensitive to group dynamics: Begin with fun and focusing icebreaker warm-ups; follow with interactive instruction (two-way substantive questions), group work (such as collective case studies or problem-solving), and experiential exercises, games, or activities; and conclude with a wrap-up to summarize the session and anticipate the next. (For well-tested samples of each, review the previous chapter.)

AIM 1: CHANGE PARTICIPANTS INTO COLLEAGUES

Few teaching experiences are scarier than your first time facing a group of strangers, some older than you, who you need to mold into a collegial team. Luckily, chances are your trainees are equally nervous, so your leadership will let both them and you feel more comfortable soon. Remember that this first, and most fundamental, aim of the entire course requires that you facilitate participants' acquaintance, sense of safety, and team spirit. Again, fortunately, you can start on these goals immediately—even before anyone shows up—through some common-sense yet very meaningful basics, presented here in their likeliest order:

Before the entire course starts, learn your learners. "Presearch" them for a rough idea of their interests and basic demographics (levels of proficiency with the topic, organization[s] they work for, ages, genders, educational level, and cultural background) from their organization or a previous instructor, so you can weave in relevant metaphors and accommodate varying language fluency. Of course, you'll adjust your pitch based on initial observations, but advance knowledge helps. Just don't let it freeze your view of trainees as they evolve.

Case in Point: The Limits of First Impressions

At the end of a course I often have participants draw a personal timeline with significant life events and present it to the group. I give examples: graduations, weddings, death dates of loved ones, first jobs, getting fired, and births of children. In a group comprised mostly of sworn law enforcement officers, speaker after speaker discussed painful, even traumatic, events. The mood was heavy and I was surprised, as people usually mention mostly joyful occasions.

When we came to the last person in the circle—a very tough, no-nonsense, high-ranking and highly concrete officer—I realized I had made a huge mistake choosing this activity. I was sure he would guffaw at such self-indulgence. Instead he said quietly, "The most significant event in my life was when I found out Santa Claus wasn't real."

His statement taught me on many levels. The person I had fixed on as the "tough guy" wasn't tough at all. Over the course of the program, he had listened, heard, and taken risks. My mistake wasn't picking this activity; it was not noticing how much of a true leader this officer had become.

Then, prepare a short but explicit syllabus with readings and assignments, along with their due dates and your overall objectives. Write in plain language without complex terms or jargon. If you're unsure what to write for your objectives, ask yourself what would show you that participants "got" each part of the material; it will tell you exactly what and how you want them to learn.

Finally, for distribution throughout the course, write (or post) module- or session-based assignment sheets with clear instructions listing resources and steps required to meet objectives. You can always supplement these later, but it will help you clarify your goals tremendously if you compose them all before the course even starts. Plus, you'll be able to accommodate class members who need to miss a future session and want to complete reading and assignments in advance. Before the first meeting, you may want to assign Part I, chapter 1, from this book, on what adult learning theory tells us about leadership training.

Before each session, make the classroom welcoming: Get there early, adjust the heat/air/windows, check the lights, remove random junk (or report serious annoyances), write the agenda (with break times) on the board, and arrange the seating in a U shape with your chair (not a desk or podium) in its "pit" to maximize your accessibility. Make eye contact with and greet each arriving participant warmly by name. It's fine to ask folks' names the first few sessions—remember, you're modeling how to get acquainted!

At the first session, introduce yourself, the course expectations, and group process: Briefly introduce yourself—as a person, not a resume—and go over your syllabus briefly; figure on spending about 10 minutes for both. This practice orients participants to you, the course environment, content, presumed skills, learning objectives, and methods of assessment. Clarify especially that their interactions with the group will enter into their individual grades.

Then, informally ask about their goals and work with them to align their aims with those you set out in the syllabus. (Note: If the course is very short or largely online, you can still introduce yourself and the syllabus by a pre-session email with your contact information, and solicit participants' ideas on course content and basic rules. You can work this data into your first session, establishing your credibility as a listener and letting class members know they're crucial in setting course expectations.) If you haven't assigned it yet, finish by assigning all or sections of Part I, chapter 1, from this book.

Once you've resolved course content, have class members discuss and set norms for basic classroom behavior (like eating and drinking, or using phones and other devices). Then, if they don't bring them up, propose and have them decide on more complex expectations, such as, "Only one person should speak at a time" or "We will be non-judgmental about people's remarks."

Remember that, as the leader, you're modeling how not to let others behave in ways you don't like, while remaining open and respectful. While most participants will be on the same page as you about basic norms, if some are not, you've got a great teaching opportunity to explain the value of 100 percent commitment to the course and colleagues. Aim to build an honest relationship with them so they will build honest relationships with each other.

Case in Point: Honesty Is the Best Policy

To give you a great example of the hazards of non-transparency and perfectionism, I confess that after a serious illness, my outsized sense of responsibility pushed me to return to teaching far too soon. I couldn't attain my usual energy level, but decided not to reveal the reason to class members. I wish I had, because in course evaluations a number of respondents marked that I was "lazy," which indicated they had felt disregard from me—ironically, the exact opposite of my exaggerated conscientiousness! I realize now that sacrificing for my supposed dignity instead of being honest totally backfired, as it usually does.

Experiential Lesson Outline to Get Participants Acquainted

During the first session, in keeping with the facilitation model, introductions will be learner-led and will acquaint trainees with each other as whole people rather than defining them by titles and achievements. Your own brief introduction will have set the tone by focusing on your personality rather than your degrees and accomplishments. The relaxed but illuminating First-Session Interviews give each participant at least one "buddy" and a nodding acquaintance with everyone from the very first session. It also lets you observe their personalities and motivations. Remember to schedule ample time to follow this (and every) activity with a debriefing. If you have time for another long activity and debriefing, add Diversity Bingo, or save it for the next session.

Experiential Lesson Outline to Build a Sense of Safety

In addition to the activities we'll mention here, you have infinite informal opportunities to foster a sense of safety. Express your commitment to a comfortable, safe learning environment and explain what that means; be the first to reveal (within bounds) a personal foible or challenge; praise respectful debate; note commonalities between class members; remark on and, if needed, halt the group "ganging up" on someone for an unpopular idea; reopen unfinished topics from the previous session; gently note role rigidity and invite participants to switch roles; and avoid talking just to folks sitting up front or who appear to agree with you—all of these behaviors make trainees feel protected and heard.

If you didn't play Diversity Bingo to acquaint participants with each other, it's equally useful for establishing a sense of safety. That's because, while giving participants unexpected information about others—a behavior that increases diversity awareness—it also lessens their personal anxiety about being different (as we all are). Follow with a debriefing. For the same reason, the Learning Style Quiz legitimates an array of study and thinking preferences, and acceptance of them again relieves individuals' fears about not fitting in. Hobby Shop also showcases unexpected and various talents in the group, which, yet again, provides a relaxing sense of inclusiveness and appreciation within the group.

Another excellent early activity, Dinner Party, asks small groups of participants to invite three exemplars of leadership to dine with them, and has the group plan the menu. This lets learners express values and creativity without having to make explicit statements that might feel risky at this stage. Figure on 30 to 40 minutes for the small-group activity, including group presentations to the whole class and debriefing as a full class. It's fun to put guest lists and menus on posterboard and compare them, and nothing enhances the sense of comfort like your bringing chocolate or candies as an extra "dessert" for all!

Experiential Lesson Outline to Encourage Teamwork

Knowing how to encourage teamwork is essential in facilitation. The first step is to remember that you're modeling teamwork. So be a team player: If you promise to do something, do it. Treat everyone fairly and don't play favorites. Solicit participants' ideas and really work to adopt them.

Especially at the beginning, you may want to organize small-group teams that balance diverse strengths—detail and big-picture thinking; speaking and research skills; creativity and critical analysis. Let the teams themselves decide the division of labor, just request that everyone have duties and deadlines, and that all team members present instead of just one representative.

Urge class members to set achievable and measurable short-term goals as well as long-term ones. With participant-driven goals and a participant-developed code of ethics, the group will begin to self-manage. Peer pressure and individual pride will help curb absenteeism, lateness, and lackadaisical commitment.

Don't panic if the group doesn't gel at first. Remember Tuckman's Five Stages (or review them in Part I, chapter 3). Groups may stay in the forming or storming stages for quite a while. Watch from a distance and see if they can resolve their differences themselves. If not, take action. Praise and reward the whole team, not just "star" members—give them good marks privately, but avoid fomenting jealousy. Recognize individuals' dedication to the team rather than their personal talents. Challenge each class member to contribute, and change their assigned responsibilities if needed.

Most importantly, be upbeat. Expect great team spirit and focus on what's going right. Reduce the number of rules and solidify the group by taking time to laugh together. Acknowledge that groups can be frustrating, but if you promote mutual respect, cooperation, and enthusiasm, you'll inspire genuine teamwork, even if not every class member displays it.

Case in Point: You Can't Always Win

To give you the benefit of my experience with the risks and rewards of facilitation, I'll tell you about a trainee I had early in my career whose advanced degree let him think himself the "expert on everything." He made lengthy, irrelevant comments until I directed him to stop, then visibly pouted, postured, and tuned out. He tried to impose his own agenda on his subgroup and met my redirection with sarcasm, challenges to my authority, and slamming the textbook loudly. Absent on one occasion, he emailed everyone in class a flurry of questions about graduation— eight months away—and blamed me for his colleague's failure to satisfy graduation requirements. Before the next session, when I confronted him about this latest disruption, he replied, "It's the class's fault they read emails in session." While some participants thanked me privately for being the only instructor to have set limits for him, no one in class opposed his conduct.

After many office-hour conversations he began to behave better, and I congratulated myself that he was finally on board. But I discovered that his barely buried anger fueled his filing a string of formal complaints about the program and me. I realized then that, while everyone can, not everyone will learn.

Now, I think I would address such a situation first in class as a case-in-point exercise, soliciting feedback about the effect of his behavior while thwarting a general attack. If the behavior continued, I would speak with the offender privately. If even that did not resolve the issue, I would not hesitate to drop her or him from the class. Either a reformation or an exile would have ended other class members' distraction and anxiety.

In explaining activities and projects, present the desired result and trust the team to develop the plan together and meet it on time. The classic Tower Building project forces individuals to plan and perform as a well-oiled machine. It also has built-in observers who will note and comment on group process in the debriefing. Another activity encouraging efficient interaction, One, Two, All, has individuals in a small group collaborate on short presentations for the whole class. Debrief after each presentation.

AIM 2: KEEP IT FACILITATIVE

The watchwords for this aim are commitment, inclusion, and contribution. Your immediate goals are to help trainees recognize their own and others' resistance, to sensitize everyone to different learning strengths in their colleagues and within themselves, and to engender lively and meaningful feedback on leadership content and process. Assigning Part I, chapter 2 of this book should prime discussion about resistance in facilitative settings.

Experiential Lesson Outline to Help Participants Identify Resistance

At this point you've already explained and assigned readings on facilitation, how it differs from traditional learning, and why it's a great approach for studying and practicing leadership. And you've helped individuals feel safe and the group coalesce. So the collectivity (including you) is now at the stage when it needs to notice, and counteract, the natural resistance we all have to new modes of behavior. And there's good reason we consider resistance natural. Facilitation makes us kick our ingrained habit of passive learning. Worse, interactive techniques demand introspection and connection, dredge up feelings, and challenge longstanding mental structures. So of course they invite resistance—from facilitators as well as participants!

Most people want to experience such opening, but fear disapproval. A few people love to dominate, so they can't tolerate respecting everyone's voice. And some have been disappointed in courses that promised interaction but quickly resorted to top-down lecturing.

Your skillful choice of relevant activities and your consistent welcoming of participant contributions should eventually change their minds. Until then, though, they may aim their negative feelings toward you, complaining that what you're asking them to do is a stupid waste of time, or following directions half-heartedly, or just ignoring them.

And you will resist, too. Inexperienced facilitators faced with group resistance often feel their own resolve slipping away. They present exercises nervously, implement them hurriedly, or abandon the interactive agenda and retreat to a lecture format. Pollack says your inner resistance will whisper this loop: "I shouldn't do this exercise because some members are too old; some members are too young; we can't move the table out of the way; the room is set up wrong; it's too hot; someone will get hurt; I'll look foolish; I don't know what to say; it's easier to skip it and move on with the agenda; people are relaxed and don't need interactive; this group has a lot to say, so they don't need to do interactive; this group is getting along well, so they don't need to do interactive; this is the wrong exercise for right now; I'll look foolish; this exercise is too silly; I'll do it next time; it's too high-risk; what if they won't do it?; we don't have time; I'm not prepared to process it; I'll look foolish . . .."

Maybe the exercise you planned is too high-risk or someone could get hurt. But to know, you need to distinguish between the voice of reason and the voice of resistance. You also need to remember that facilitation is not about your own comfort—so what if you do look foolish?—it's about creating an effective environment for the group to meet its goals.

But don't despair. You'll gradually recognize and work through your own fears, which is necessary for addressing your trainees' fears. And when you persevere in overcoming your own resistance and get skilled with interactive techniques, you'll begin to see concrete results, including profound changes in individuals' behavior and significant jumps in the group's cohesion. So learn to live with eternal resistance in the group and in you. You'll soon see resistance as a sign of success, not failure. In fact, you'll eventually welcome it as proof to show the group that something important is happening.

Case in Point: You Don't Have to be Perfect

Despite my best efforts at encouraging collegiality, two trainees developed a furious enmity and asked me to move one of them out of their subgroup. I generally ask participants to work out their difficulties as part of learning about group process, but in this instance I reassigned one to another group, rationalizing that "I'm their teacher, not their therapist." But I soon felt angry at myself for having erred. About a year later, I heard from alums that the pair had made peace and had actually become great friends. So my mistake turned out to be the right call. I'd really love to think my inspiring instruction finally sunk in, making this a teachable moment in retrospect. But I honestly still think I was wrong— and I have come to be alright with that.

More practically, by dealing with resistance the moment you notice it, you lower hostility to the point where resistant class members at least cease to disrupt others. But if trainees have to suppress their resentment, it will follow you throughout the course. Your goal is to deal with resistance while respecting the resistant. You may—diplomatically and without shaming—remark on people's hostile or withdrawing body language and invite them to express their feelings verbally. Invite group members to talk about their difficulties coming to the course, or to express their outrage at having been required to come. Acknowledge the anger, and assure the group that talking about resistance is a useful leadership lesson.

If you've been following this guide, you've already discussed class norms and settled on them as a group. However, a participant or two may flout those decisions by talking out of turn, texting during presentations, or disrespecting colleagues. As noted in previous chapters, you'll have to manage truly serious infractions, but most behavioral problems stemming from resistance can and should be handled collectively. A great section for the class to read now is "Group Dynamics in Your Classroom" from Part I, chapter 3. Of course, you'll alert trainees that whenever the current manual refers to "you, the facilitator," they should think of it as "you, the leader." Asking them why may itself spark a great discussion!

If you've been keeping the classroom physically comfortable and reasonably private, the group members feeling emotionally safe, and everyone involved in decisions on curriculum and decorum, you've already started facilitating the group's self-governance. Open the discussion by asking someone to recall for the class what it does and does not tolerate, and why. Then introduce comments about the different ways people resist group expectations, and characterize such behaviors as assertive, passive, aggressive, or passive-aggressive. Of course, as the instructor you should model emotional health through your awareness and openness about personal triggers. This will help you, and by extension your trainees, keep individual issues separate from those of the class as a whole, while allowing everyone to discuss and manage group dynamics.

As an informal way to head off resistance take the group's "temperature" regularly by inquiring, "Does everyone understand?" or "Any questions, concerns, or comments?" These periodic check-ups advertise your desire to involve participants as much as possible. If you truly hear what they say, it's unlikely they'll highjack the question to derail the course in futile discussions about objectives, agenda, or content.

The classic organizational exercise Company Town challenges participants to follow rules, commit to their teams, and contribute their best efforts, so anyone's failure to do so will become readily apparent. Follow with a debriefing and be sure to include questions about group members' participation and general attitude. Another excellent cooperative exercise, You're on Your Own, also favors team-playing; debriefing should explore the potential costs of competitiveness.

Experiential Lesson Outline to Demonstrate Varied Learning Preferences

Before you can sensitize participants to their and others' personal learning styles, know your own teaching style. Do you favor whole-class discussions or small groups? Do you deliver content complete with audio and animation, black and white overheads, PowerPoint, a chalkboard, or a video? In your classroom do people sit, draw, or move?

Even if you think participants are getting the main ideas, it's valuable to present them in different ways so all learners can grasp them with equal ease. Accommodating the many ways of knowing—intuitive, rational, kinesthetic, visual, and auditory—lets your teaching "click" for everyone. Very small modifications dramatically expand the accessibility of your teaching style. For instance, when you present, use clear, concise phrases instead of acronyms or technical jargon unless absolutely necessary. Invite your trainees to catch you and anyone using acronyms or jargon in class without first defining the terms, so everyone remembers to value one's audience over one's vocabulary.

Have class members review differentiated instruction (Part I, chapter 2). Then, if you haven't done so earlier, ask them to take an online Learning Style Quiz out of class, in pairs or small groups, and discuss the experience in the next session. They'll gain both self-knowledge and an appreciation of the variety of intelligences. Best of all, it's fun—and often relieving—for learners to know that they're primarily auditory, visual, or kinesthetic thinkers. And you'll get an idea of the kinds of thinkers populating your course, so you can pitch your presentations more effectively.

Let Gardner's Multiple Intelligence Theory inspire you to enrich your teaching by trying new slants: In addition to traditionally favored verbal-linguistic and logical-mathematical intelligences, be sure to honor aesthetic understanding, self-awareness, physical know-how, cooperative learning, psychological wisdom, musical skill, reflection, visualization, and storytelling ability. Make your teaching work for those thinking characteristics by including tasks for the active (hands-on, group, and problem-solving activities); the reflective (solo work, ample time to "digest" information, and thoughtful summaries); the sensing (concrete details, facts, procedures, and applications rather than abstract theory); the intuitive (interrelationships, new concepts, and interpretation); and the sequential (logical steps, linear format, and material broken down into smaller chunks).

Another great way you can incorporate multiple ways of knowing is to juggle media—go from mini-lecture to activity to movie clips (or YouTube) to having participants move around. By the way, just standing up raises the heart-rate, sends more blood to the brain, activates the central nervous system, and increases neural firing. So whenever you think your learners' energy drops, have them stand or stroll for a few minutes.

Tailor your study skills guidance to different learning orientations. Counsel auditory learners to recite aloud the main points of a textbook or lecture, study with a friend, review audiotapes of classroom proceedings, pronounce new vocabulary and definitions out loud, and record their class notes to listen to later. Advise visual learners to take creative notes—you can even keep butcher paper and colored pencils readily accessible in class. These folks probably took notes this way all through school, but may have been punished for "doodling."

Incorporate meaningful pictures, diagrams, charts, timelines, concept maps, videos, and demonstrations in your teaching whenever possible. Encourage visual thinkers to draw, build, and design for their projects and to preview chapters by first looking at subheadings and illustrations.

Since facilitation embraces learning differences, your course presents endless opportunities for individualized and multisensory work. Musical or rhythmic learners can write content-rich raps and perform them for the class. A drum circle or a musical jam with simple instruments can enhance group cohesion and listening skills. Interpersonally oriented participants can use their communication gifts to survey colleagues and report their findings. Individualistic thinkers can create original projects (subject to your approval) and work alone on a class presentation. Kinesthetic, hands-on learners can take notes on flip charts, stand while reading, and present stories, skits, and role plays. Logical/mathematical thinkers can demonstrate experiments, crunch numbers, categorize and classify abstract patterns. Utilizing all these talents gives the class a variety of insights and trains them to appreciate and synthesize differing viewpoints—a prime leadership talent.

In addition to activating all these intelligences, your facilitative course should include a mix of instructor-participant interaction (presentations and responses, and feedback on assignments); participant-participant interaction (introduction exercises, group discussion and projects, and peer critiques); and participant-content interaction (essays, term papers, and individual projects).

If you haven't used it yet, Hobby Shop experientially conveys the truth that different people think differently, and is a fun way for class members to get to know each other more deeply. Of course, let your debriefing questions following each presentation stress the presenter's unique skills and ability to demonstrate them.

Experiential Lesson Outline to Generate Discussion

Just as you need to confront resistance continuously, you always need to engage and re-engage attention and interest—again, starting with you, since nothing is more contagious (and sometimes, perishable) than enthusiasm. Specific presentation techniques help. To start, ask open-ended questions that engage your learners in thinking and feeling, changing their brains from passive to active mode. Open such engagement questions with a short video clip, an intriguing photograph, or a class opinion poll. Embedding questions in your presentations keeps learners on track by reviewing material and providing immediate feedback on their answers. And during sessions, send participants on a "treasure hunt" through a source or website with a list of questions as their guide.

For the same reason you pose questions, use humor to enliven interactions and support learning (but never to marginalize a sector, wound an individual, or entertain the crowd—that's not the kind of attention you want or the techniques you want to model!). Relevant humor keeps learners relaxed and alert, and laughter releases adrenaline and other neurotransmitters, which increases long-term retention of information. Other focus-grabbers include giving the inside scoop on an issue important to your learners (whose interests you know by now) and throwing in a personal story that gives you credibility and connects to the group emotionally.

Facilitation offers many ways to spark (or re-spark) attention, because it's founded on participant interests. You're already enlivening the start of each class with icebreakers that create an open and pleasant environment and encourage involvement. Add in-class or posted icebreakers, such as "Why I'm Taking This Course" or "My Three-Sentence Autobiography." Focused case studies, which can take as little as five minutes or absorb weeks, work equally in classroom or virtual instruction, because many information sources are online and an increasing number of professions use the Internet as a primary resource and communication venue.

A debate can also ignite a session. You may wish to use a structured forum until the class is cohesive enough to govern itself: Give each side a specific time period in which to construct an argument (say, 10 minutes). Then allow each side 10 minutes to construct a rebuttal. After one or two rounds of civil rebuttals, compliment the group's diplomacy, and tell them you're opening up the forum for free-form debates. This exercise can also be conducted online, with members posting their arguments and ripostes.

Having learners present current events or review films or TV shows revealing good or bad leadership, and then relating them to their own organizational lives, makes for vivacious conversation. The Two-Minute Paper and Movie Night activities (each followed with a debriefing) engender lively commentary as well. (Movie Night will work equally for later lesson outlines on the experience of leadership, and there are so many great films you can use this activity more than once.) Have participants finish reading and discuss Part I, chapter 3, reminding them again that "you, the facilitator," also means "you, the leader."

AIM 3: DEMONSTRATE LEADERSHIP TRANSACTIONS
Experiential Lesson Outline to Approach Leadership Readings

Your increasingly cohesive group setting will make reading truly engaging—perhaps for the first time, for many—if you help trainees frame the readings in the context of their own experience. Facilitative education gets participants to reflect, to turn the light of their observations back onto themselves. Briefly elicit the main points of the readings, then get participants to pull examples from their own lives and careers that confirm or challenge those points. In addition to discussion, you can use individual journaling or art to allow reflection on written material. Experiment with giving different groups identical readings to study and present—as each group perceives the text in a unique way, different aspects of the material get covered and participants see a vivid example of people's distinctive filters.

First, assign Part II about measuring the effectiveness of facilitative training of leaders in private and public sectors, again reminding the trainees that "leader" should be substituted in their minds for "facilitator" in the text. Once those basics are mastered, many other works can draw participants to further self-reflection: *Looking Out, Looking In* by Adler and Proctor lifts readers' awareness of communication and relationship. The classic *Learning to Lead* by Bennis and Goldsmith focuses on reflection and building leadership skills—have participants complete the workbook and go over it with them. Learners also react profoundly to Quinn's *Deep Change* and Frankl's inspiring *Man's Search for Meaning*. Other books promoting reflection include Goleman's *Emotional Intelligence* books and Covey's *The Seven Habits of Highly Effective People*. Assign carefully written reflections on any of these, which participants may let you share or have you keep confidential.

Experiential Lesson Outline on Experiences of Leadership

As you and your class know from earlier chapters, your leadership itself teaches leadership, much the way that good parents model the maturity they want their kids to attain (to review this idea, see "The Big Secret: Interactive Learning Requires Relationships" in Part I, chapter 2, and "The Medium Is the Message" in Part I, chapter 3). Although earlier you functioned as the acknowledged leader, if you're meeting your aims you'll increasingly see, and celebrate, the group's internalization of the executive powers you've demonstrated. Again like a good parent, you may now need to avoid doing for the group what it can, even if imperfectly, do for itself. And, most important, if you've encouraged participants to support each other, they'll have freed themselves from needing your approval—thereby winning it all the more!

The Leadership Photo Collage activity capitalizes on the increased alertness of the group to executive issues all around them. Done in pairs or small groups, this project exercises the cooperative creativity at the heart of great leadership. In addition to picking and discussing the photos, have course members explore the process of conceptualizing, planning, and creating the collages in your whole-class debriefing. Reading Part II on evaluating facilitative leadership training in private and public sectors forms a useful companion to this activity.

A favorite technique of art therapists, Projective Drawing lets trainees literally see their growth. By the latter part of the course, members should feel comfortable enough to depict and describe internal states, but be sure to follow with an especially sensitive debriefing. As you might have guessed, this activity particularly engages visual and kinesthetic thinkers, but mathematical/logical learners can surprise you as they foray into an unfamiliar medium and present deeply felt insights.

You might have used Movie Night earlier to generate discussion, but here you could use it specifically to identify and critique leadership styles. Schedule ample time to discuss disturbing elements in the films before you screen them and what may be a lengthy debriefing afterward.

Case in Point: Prepare the Soil

In one course, there were three female officers who banded together in continual side conversations, impervious to my correction. So I shouldn't have been surprised that my showing the movie about the improbable football hero, Rudy, seemed to give them a green light to complain that this story could never have happened and therefore I didn't know what I was teaching. Only a classmate's confirming the film's accuracy silenced them—so much so that they never participated in class again.

In a similar scenario, one enrollee was outraged at my having shown the classic leadership movie on African American soldiers in the Civil War, *Glory*, because of its use of the N-word—a sad but unquestionably accurate touch. Although it certainly fired up our debriefing debate on the relativity or universality of ethics, I stood by my choice of this and other difficult films. But I learned from these instances to preface disturbing movies (such as these two and the Holocaust film, *Conspiracy*) with especially careful discussion, and to debrief group reactions thoroughly afterward.

Experiential Lesson Outline on Cognitive, Affective, and Behavioral Responses to the Leadership Course

Having studied examples of executive skills in the world and practiced them in the course, participants can now consider how they have, or would, incorporate leadership skills into their own professional and personal lives. Whether formal or informal, a Personal Development Plan designed by each class member—as a rap, video, poem, or essay—encourages reflection on his or her internal process throughout the course. Have participants share these with the class, and let each design and lead a debriefing after his or her presentation.

In addition, you may have each participant create a Vision Statement. This assignment provides practice in visioning—imagining long-term goals before designing short-term objectives to achieve them—and clarifies individuals' personal and professional aims in view of their strengths and weaknesses— another crucial leadership ability.

Again relying on your trainees' leadership expertise, have individuals utilize their observational and communication skills to analyze groups in the real world by completing Paging Dr. Freud. Follow presentations with a debriefing.

AIM 4: HELP PARTICIPANTS RECONCILE DIFFERING VIEWS
Teaching Participants to Listen, Check, and Mirror

You've doubtless noticed recently that participants have been taking on more and more of "your" job: They support and, if needed, discipline each other; they lead discussions; they present content to the class; and they reflect on group and their inner process. And that means you're doing your job! (You may also have noticed that this guide needs to guide you less.) Now you can teach your trainees to hone their skill at capturing others' ideas and bring it up to your level—a necessary step for developing leaders. Throughout the course you've modeled active listening by double-checking and mirroring what others have expressed. You've put vague statements into your own words, asked, "Have I got it right?" and adjusted as needed, then restated.

But the active listening you've been demonstrating yields more than an accurate report on someone else's words and feelings. It also trains your own mind to attend fully to what's going on, rather than to drift. Active listening means listening with a purpose: to gain information, understand others, solve problems, share interest, or show support. It's much harder than talking, as it requires the receiver to hear, understand, verify, and give feedback. Active listening also exercises relational skills: You listen more than you talk, you don't interrupt, you don't finish others' sentences, you note your biases, you don't let your mind wander to your own preoccupations, and you summarize accurately before judging. Model these leadership skills, and watch your trainees practice and polish them!

The Detectives activity gives participants practice in active listening by forcing them to clarify separate statements and unify them into a small-group project. Trust class members to do this on their own, and follow with a debriefing on how it felt.

Teaching Participants the Art of Give and Take

As you near culmination, your final lessons will guide emerging executives to harmonize all the leadership theories, learning styles, and transforming personal opinions they've experienced throughout the course. In fact, both they and you have a lot of new ideas to incorporate. Lucky for you all, facilitation weaves varied intellectual and emotional strands into a unified fabric.

One of the most powerful methods of integrating leadership lessons, and one of the most fun, has the group plan and carry out its own graduation party. Although it can seem silly or too basic, Graduation Party Planning requires finely negotiated, collaborative decisions about division of labor, finances, theme, decorations, dress code, guest policy, venue, and menu. Any group that can pull all that off and have fun doing it certainly deserves to graduate—thanks to you!

Case in Point: Group Accountability

Participants in a new cohort of sworn police officers rolled their eyes when told, "Plan your graduation party together." They refused to take this "waste of time" seriously, and needed constant goading to negotiate entertainment, venue, decorations, menu, location, time, theme, and countless details. But I stuck to my guns. And that experience of consensus-building enabled the classmates to create a month-by-month agenda and follow it throughout their two-and-a-half-year program.

In the process, this cohort became each other's facilitators. Once I used the classic art therapy technique, Projective Drawing, and had everyone sketch two self-portraits: the first, of themselves at work, and the second, of themselves at home. When someone left his work portrait perfectly blank, a classmate censured his "disrespectful resistance." The trainee defended himself—his current assignment was top secret!

Teaching Participants to Monitor Their Audience

You've already introduced your trainees to the concept of monitoring their listeners when you made them stop their presentations—or yours—to define overly complex terms or jargon. And they've observed your diplomatic remarking on class member's body language and inviting them to express their feelings verbally. Now your task is explicitly to sharpen their observation skills to read, and thus better engage, their own audience. Before class members give presentations, remind them to attend to nonverbal as well as verbal messages, to use eye contact to connect, and to avoid reliance on PowerPoint or notes. Make it real by having peers evaluate each other as speakers and explain their judgments in a general debriefing.

You can now ask participants to do exactly what you've been doing by having them fill out Course Evaluations. Urge them to use what they've learned and experienced in the course to pin down exactly what a teacher, speaker, leader must know about, and give to, his or her class, audience, or organization. After the evaluations have been collected, enjoy a last, excellent debriefing. Expect a satisfying sense of closure—tinged with healthy nostalgia—to this interactive transformation of randomly assorted individuals into an efficient and ethical executive team. (For assessments by alums and their supervisors, and texts of longitudinal, cumulative, and multi-population surveys, see Part II, chapter 5, and the Appendix.)

REFLECTION AND NEXT STEPS

1. **Consider your feelings.** Did you find this chapter relieving or did it make you anxious about teaching using the facilitative approach? What parts of it made you feel most confident and eager to get started? How can you use those sections to help you enjoy teaching this way?

2. **Consider your learners' feelings.** Do you think your trainees feel any anxiety about your leadership development course? What might they be uncomfortable with? How can you best put them at their ease and encourage active participation?

3. **Rank your teaching goals.** Of all the teaching aims mentioned in this chapter, which do you find most important? Least important? How would you link those less-central points to the most central ones to make the whole course meaningful?

REFERENCES AND RESOURCES

Adler, R., and R. Proctor. (2013). *Looking Out, Looking In*, 14th edition. Boston: Wadsworth.

Bennis, W., and J. Goldsmith. (1994). *Learning to Lead: A Workbook on Becoming a Leader*. Reading, MA: Addison-Wesley Publishing.

Cherniss, C., and D. Goleman. (editors). (2001). *The Emotionally Intelligent Workplace: How to Select for, Measure, and Improve Emotional Intelligence in Individuals, Groups, and Organizations*. San Francisco: Jossey-Bass.

Covey, S.R. (1989). *The Seven Habits of Highly Effective People*. New York: Simon and Schuster.

Frankl, V. (1959/2006). *Man's Search for Meaning. An Introduction to Logotherapy*. Boston: Beacon Press.

Goleman, D. (1996). *Emotional Intelligence: Why it Can Matter More Than IQ*. New York: Bantam Books.

Goleman, D. (1998). *Working With Emotional Intelligence*. New York: Bantam Books.

Goleman, D., R. Boyatzis, and A. McKee. (2001). "Primal Leadership: The Hidden Driver of Great Performance." *Harvard Business Review*, 79(11): 42-51.

Pollack, S. "Moving Beyond Icebreakers: An Innovative Approach to Group Facilitation, Learning, and Action," www.movingbeyondicebreakers.org/chapters/coping-with-re sistance.php (accessed July 24, 2013).

Quinn, R. (1996). *Deep Change: Discovering the Leader Within*. San Francisco: Jossey-Bass.

Chapter 8
Wrapping It Up

Well, now you've read it all and are ready to put the facilitative training of leaders into effect. But before you embark headlong on that adventure, let's recap the main points of this manual, step-by-step. The adult education, group dynamics, and leadership studies content of the course—the substance you need to impart to trainees—might be found in most traditional executive skills courses. It's the facilitative manner in which you impart it that elevates your course from passive listening to active, deep, hands-on, and lasting learning—and challenges you in the process.

ADULT LEARNING

First, recall that adult learning studies show that mature people continue to evolve in their learning capacities, and ultimately attain the cognitive level of creative problem-solving that is superior to the final stage in classic developmental theory. But the never-ending growth of mental power also means that adult students do not share a uniform mode of thinking. On the contrary, mature learners display as much variety in learning preferences as young people do, and these preferences may continue to shift throughout life. So your trainees will require all the same differentiated, individually-tailored teaching techniques used in pedagogy—verbal, non-verbal, visual, kinesthetic, auditory, and reflective.

What older learners do share, however, is their interest in the immediate applicability and job- or life-relevance of the material. They generally also display the ability to work with other learners, as long as the work taps into their own motivations. Cooperative, participant-led, and hands-on, facilitation combines the strengths of many adult education approaches. As such it superbly transforms learners into leaders by providing real-time practice in clarifying one's own vision, comprehending others' thinking, and setting and achieving collective goals. By giving trainees maximum say on course aims, organization, and assessment, you as a leadership facilitator actually exercise their independent, flexible leadership skills. Those talents are more than personal and theoretical; they're interactive, consensus-building group experiences that are practiced and deeply learned in real time, with real colleagues—just like real business and real life. You're gradually guiding them away from the authority of a boss or a group (or you!) to rely on their own innovative, applicable, and ethical wisdom to blend individual and organizational interests. And not only do you need to keep all this in mind as a facilitator; your executive trainees need to comprehend this about the adults they will one day lead, and be able to foster the very same self-awareness and collaborative energy in them.

CREATING A FACILITATIVE CLASSROOM

Ironically, when we teach leadership in a facilitative manner we're really creating an egalitarian, cooperative community of leaders. That's rarely done in the typical classroom—not to mention in private enterprise. Yet establishing a safe, open, supportive, and intensely engaging environment ranks not just as your first, but as your most important task as a leadership facilitator.

Thoughtful organization of your classroom and session time goes a long way to removing physical and temporal barriers to universal participation. Avoid the usual pulpit-and-pews or assigned-seats layout and explicitly carve out time for everyone's comments. In your own remarks, differentiate your presentations to match as many learning preferences as possible: visual, verbal, auditory, and active. Even more important, tailor your teaching to the expressed interests of the group; you'll be modeling responsiveness and openness, and you'll keep learners involved. At the same time, be honest with participants and don't let the difficult ones bully others, or you, into offensive or excluding actions and speech. You're the leader now, but you're leading them to establish responsible, inclusive partnerships with all participants, including yourself. You do that by demonstrating, identifying, and debating leader-like qualities and holding your trainees to the same standards: respecting self and others, supporting everyone's growth, and being reliable.

Being that kind of a leader isn't just a good idea. It's critical to the life of the learning community you're building. The psychological rigors of participant-led education strain teachers and trainees, and both parties will find themselves defying its demands. Only a fully cohesive group can weather its own resistance and survive the challenges and discomforts of truly transformational experience. That cohesiveness starts with you, and grows from your ethical stance. Unless you behave with honesty and genuine care, your trainees will never come to trust you—and thus to trust each other—and you'll be back to the lecturing found in traditional classrooms: a superficially comfortable, but ultimately useless, method for training real leaders. In effect, you'll be conveying the very opposite of the content you're professing, and will end up with power-based, distant, irresponsible heads of companies instead of collaborative, involved, ethical executives.

LEARNING AND TEACHING GROUP DYNAMICS

As it happens, one of the best ways to craft a learning community and teach future leaders what they need to build their own teams is to learn together about groups. Every business or service organization constitutes a group, so understanding the mechanisms of its collective functioning provides crucial insight to anyone attempting to lead it. Better than the most deeply researched dissertation, the immediate experience of your classroom will teach participants about the different types of groups and the many roles, explicit or underground, that group members play. More important, it will instruct them in a hands-on, hearts-on way they'll take with them into their work life—and home life.

Learning through experience how to recognize, manage, and—with skill and luck—transform difficult group members will probably rank as the most valuable knowledge you can impart. In addition you'll teach your trainees how to assess the health of entire groups by evaluating their functioning. They'll learn to recognize not just the obvious states of cohesion or factionalism; they'll be able to tell if the collectivity completes tasks synergistically, or rubber-stamps every decision by groupthink. But even more important than such diagnostic skills, under your guidance your participant-led community of future leaders will have themselves lived, and thus learned, how to address glitches in group performance. And that's because they'll see how their class formed, fought, and ultimately bonded to complete the common agenda through the united talents of its individual members.

It's in that experience that the value of values—the centrality of trustworthiness to leadership—becomes apparent to participants. At this point not just your modeling of high ethical standards, but your trainees' practicing them, will sharpen their executive powers. And that kind of experiential education will make the course readings, assignments, projects, activities, and presentations come alive and stick.

GRADING FACILITATIVE TRAINING FOR PRIVATE- AND PUBLIC- SECTOR LEADERS

The longitudinal and multi-demographic surveys I took of public-sector alumni from my leadership courses, and of their supervisors, strongly suggest that facilitative training strengthened leadership skills that were applicable in the workplace and in personal life. But since no such survey or reliable inquiry has been made into the worth of facilitative leadership training in the business world—indeed, in the absence of accord on the definition of good leadership itself—there's no proof that this approach would succeed in the private sector.

Yet, as you'll teach your participants, we can draw many lessons from the challenges I faced, and overcame, in getting toughened cops from a paramilitary culture to transform themselves through the participant-led, reflective, and emotive exercise of facilitation. To make this approach work with this demographic required, first, acknowledging the sources of resistance to this manner of teaching; then, consciously tailoring the work to address such difficulties and to support the trainees' specific motivations. Of course, participants in the business sector will not display those same issues and interests. They'll display others. And that's just the point! The power of facilitative training of leaders lies in its sensitivity to, and embrace of, differences between organizations. By discussing the survey material your trainees will learn that, if it can be made to apply so successfully to police employees, it can accommodate any organizational culture.

In addition, your discussion will awaken them to the point that private enterprises have quantifiable instruments to judge the success of their training programs, which the public sector lacks. Besides customer complaints and surveys, by following trade publication reviews and tracking actual sales, corporations may gauge the value of their training through financial consequences. So the business world can learn from the public sector that facilitative training of leaders operates brilliantly when it comprehends, and creatively confronts, the organizational culture engendering participants' problems and incentives.

TRIED AND TRUE

Once you get the value of facilitative training of leaders, you're ready to learn the tricks of the trade: engaging projects and activities with full instructions and scripts, ways to evaluate individual and group work, and video and print resources and how to use them. But perhaps most useful, you get to learn from my cache of verbatim participant reactions to all of these. So you'll have advance warning of both the hazards and the hopes that experiential leadership education techniques hold.

By now you're also ready for some practical guidelines for your own performance in presenting information, managing group conflict, accomplishing the common agenda, and maintaining participant involvement. Amazingly enough, you'll find that your on-the-ground skills put into effect exactly what you've been teaching your trainees and witnessing in your classroom: that the facilitative training of leaders rests on the solidity of your integrity, initiative, and respect for self and others. That's because these exercises, as much as any executive decision they'll ever make, manifest your trainees' characters. Your recognizing this fact, and guiding participants to that realization, constitutes the essence of leadership education. As they enact and reflect upon these resources, games, and activities with your supportive but straightforward feedback, they will be storing up the self-awareness and the ethical attitudes you represent, along with the substantive material on adult learning, group dynamics, and leadership theory.

STRUCTURING FACILITATIVE SESSIONS

Armed with a host of warm-ups, readings, exercises, projects, and games, you can now consider how and when to deploy them. Depending on your class's phase of group development, you'll choose experiential activities that help members become acquainted; set behavioral and academic norms; relax; bond;

form a common agenda; challenge, encourage, and appreciate each other; and ultimately take charge of their own learning. Most crucial, in doing so you're educating them experientially in the process they'll use as leaders: supporting a random assortment of adults as they become—under skilled guidance—a productive collectivity.

Along the way you'll manage difficult individuals and group processes—and help them manage participants on their own as an executive team. You'll coach them to identify their own and peers' resistance, and even recognize, admit to, and resolve your own. You'll discover, and teach, how to vary your style to engage the widest range of learners. These experiences, while never wholly predictable, unfold in roughly expected patterns. Using experiential lesson outlines will help you navigate the incompletely charted waters of the facilitative approach to leadership education.

As you lead participants through the successive stages of group development you'll also be instructing them in increasingly sophisticated concepts of leadership. And, with the experiential vocabulary to express it—individual and collective memories of good or poor leadership, of inclusion or exclusion, of group productivity or paralysis—your trainees will learn to evaluate their own executive abilities and assess how, and how well, the course fostered them. More important, by the final stage of your instruction they will have grasped, and practiced, what you've been teaching: the art of listening to others' viewpoints, restating them accurately, and accommodating them within a shared agenda. Their accomplishment of this crucial give-and-take outlook will be your finest accomplishment as a teacher.

SUMMARY

Wrapping it up has brought us full circle to our beginning. Great facilitative training starts from your honoring your own and your learners' life experience and emotional intelligence. Creating safety and honesty in your teaching environment will allow those mature gifts to come to the fore, despite the anxiety that participant-led education can elicit. Indeed, following the findings of research into adult teaching, the facilitative approach best fosters the growth of independent, practical, responsible executive wisdom. Remember the first rule of facilitation: Know yourself, and know your trainees; then you'll know when to direct and when to accept as you watch your learners transform themselves into leaders.

Appendix

Effectiveness Surveys on the Facilitative Training of Leaders

PARTICIPANT PROGRAM EVALUATION

Please indicate your level of agreement with the following statements:

1. Overall Satisfaction:

   a. The length of the courses was:

   ❑ Too Short   ❑ Somewhat Short   ❑ Just Right

   ❑ Somewhat Long   ❑ Too Long

   b. The workload was:

   ❑ Too Light   ❑ Somewhat Light   ❑ Just Right

   ❑ Somewhat Heavy   ❑ Too Heavy

   c. I am satisfied with my experience in [NAME of PROGRAM or COURSE].

   ❑ Strongly Disagree   ❑ Disagree   ❑ Neutral

   ❑ Agree   ❑ Strongly Agree

d. How many people have you referred to the program/course?

_____

2. Because of this program/course:

    a. I am better able to handle conflict at work.
    ❑ Strongly Disagree ❑ Disagree ❑ Neutral
    ❑ Agree ❑ Strongly Agree

    b. I am a more effective employee.
    ❑ Strongly Disagree ❑ Disagree ❑ Neutral
    ❑ Agree ❑ Strongly Agree

    c. I have implemented new policies and plans.
    ❑ Strongly Disagree ❑ Disagree ❑ Neutral
    ❑ Agree ❑ Strongly Agree

    d. I am better able to manage my personal life.
    ❑ Strongly Disagree ❑ Disagree ❑ Neutral
    ❑ Agree ❑ Strongly Agree

3. As a result of this program/course, I have improved:

    a. My critical-thinking skills (collecting and analyzing information).
    ❑ Strongly Disagree ❑ Disagree ❑ Neutral
    ❑ Agree ❑ Strongly Agree

    b. My creative problem-solving skills.
    ❑ Strongly Disagree ❑ Disagree ❑ Neutral
    ❑ Agree ❑ Strongly Agree

c. My understanding of the way I make decisions.

❑ Strongly Disagree ❑ Disagree ❑ Neutral

❑ Agree ❑ Strongly Agree

d. My writing skills.

❑ Strongly Disagree ❑ Disagree ❑ Neutral

❑ Agree ❑ Strongly Agree

e. My speaking skills.

❑ Strongly Disagree ❑ Disagree ❑ Neutral

❑ Agree ❑ Strongly Agree

f. My ability to deal with people through increased awareness of cultural issues.

❑ Strongly Disagree ❑ Disagree ❑ Neutral

❑ Agree ❑ Strongly Agree

g. My responsiveness to community needs.

❑ Strongly Disagree ❑ Disagree ❑ Neutral

❑ Agree ❑ Strongly Agree

4. Work Information:

Please list any promotions or transfers you have received as a result of this program/course.

a. Assignment: _____

Classification: _____

Date: ___/____/20____

Lateral Transfer   Promotion   Other: _____

   b. Assignment: _____

   Classification: _____

   Date: ___/____/20___

   Lateral Transfer   Promotion   Other: _____

5.   Other:

   a. What did you find most valuable about the program/course?

   _____

   _____

   b. What did you find least valuable about the program/course?

   _____

   _____

   c. What would you change?

   _____

   _____

ALUMNI PROGRAM EVALUATION

Dear Graduate:

You completed the [NAME of PROGRAM/COURSE]. Your confidential response to this brief survey will help us assess and improve this training, and is very much appreciated. This survey is absolutely anonymous. The record kept of your responses will not contain any identifying information about you, and no one will ever know which answers you gave.

Feel free to contact me with any questions you may have. Thank you for your assistance.

Sincerely,

[NAME, TITLE, ORGANIZATION, AND CONTACT INFORMATION]

Please provide your
    1.   Gender

        a. Male

        b. Female

    2.   Age _____

3. Highest academic level completed:

   a. some college

   b. college graduate

   c. some post-graduate

   d. MA, MS, pastoral degree, or counseling license

   e. some doctoral

   f. PhD or other doctoral degree

4. Current title or rank:

   _____

   _____

5. Did the program/course seem different from other college or training classes in . . .

   a. the subject matter? ❑ yes ❑ no

   b. the teaching style? ❑ yes ❑ no

   c. participants' roles in class? ❑ yes ❑ no

6. Did the program/course seem different from other police training courses in . . .

   a. the subject matter? ❑ yes ❑ no

   b. the teaching style? ❑ yes ❑ no

   c. participants' roles in class? ❑ yes ❑ no

7. What do you think was unique about the program/course?

   _____

   _____

8. Did you find it difficult to get used to the classes?

    ❑ very   ❑ somewhat   ❑ not at all

9. Did any of the participants seem to dislike the classes?

    ❑ a lot   ❑ somewhat   ❑ not at all

10. Did any of the participants seem uncomfortable during the classes?

    ❑ very   ❑ somewhat   ❑ not at all

11. Did any of the participants want to avoid activities in the classes?

    ❑ very   ❑ somewhat   ❑ not at all

12. Did you find any of the following program/course activities irrelevant?

    a. Working in groups ❑ yes   ❑ no
    b. Having participants decide course goals ❑ yes   ❑ no
    c. Not getting the answers from the instructor ❑ yes   ❑ no
    d. Having to resolve participants' various opinions ❑ yes   ❑ no
    e. Having to talk about inner feelings ❑ yes   ❑ no
    f. Other:

    _____

    _____

13. Did you find any of the following program/course activities challenging?

   a. Working in groups ❑ yes ❑ no

   b. Having participants decide course goals ❑ yes ❑ no

   c. Not getting the answers from the instructor ❑ yes ❑ no

   d. Having to resolve participants' various opinions ❑ yes ❑ no

   e. Having to talk about inner feelings ❑ yes ❑ no

   f. Other:

   _____

   _____

14. Did you find any of the following program/course activities uncomfortable?

   a. Working in groups ❑ yes ❑ no

   b. Having participants decide course goals ❑ yes ❑ no

   c. Not getting the answers from the instructor ❑ yes ❑ no

   d. Having to resolve participants' various opinions ❑ yes ❑ no

   e. Having to talk about inner feelings ❑ yes ❑ no

   f. Other:

   _____

   _____

15. Did participants seem to get more comfortable with class activities over time?

   ❑ very   ❑ somewhat   ❑ not at all

16. Did class activities help participants feel they were part of a team?

   ❑ very   ❑ somewhat   ❑ not at all

17. Did you feel more connected to other participants by the end of the class?

    ❑ very   ❑ somewhat   ❑ not at all

18. Did you feel more confident by the end of the program/course?

    ❑ a lot   ❑ somewhat   ❑ not at all

19. Do you think you witnessed good leadership in the program/course?

    ❑ a lot   ❑ somewhat   ❑ not at all

20. Do you think you practiced good leadership in the program/course?

    ❑ a lot   ❑ somewhat   ❑ not at all

21. What surprised you during the program/course experience?

    _____

    _____

22. Do you feel that the program/course helped you earn a promotion or desired transfer? ❑ yes   ❑ no

23. Do you feel that the program/course helped you gain respect from fellow officers? (For private sector, omit FELLOW OFFICERS and insert colleagues.) ❑ yes   ❑ no

24. In your work with colleagues, do you feel that the program/course helped you . . .

    a. Feel more confident in your leadership abilities.

    ❑ a lot   ❑ somewhat   ❑ not at all

b. Develop or accept new ideas.

❑ a lot ❑ somewhat ❑ not at all

c. Communicate your own ideas.

❑ a lot ❑ somewhat ❑ not at all

d. Understand other points of view.

❑ a lot ❑ somewhat ❑ not at all

e. Resolve disputes.

❑ a lot ❑ somewhat ❑ not at all

f. Solve problems.

❑ a lot ❑ somewhat ❑ not at all

g. Set and achieve group goals.

❑ a lot ❑ somewhat ❑ not at all

h. Other:

_____

_____

25. In your work with the community, do you feel that the program/ course helped you . . .

a. Feel more confident in your leadership abilities.

❑ a lot ❑ somewhat ❑ not at all

b. Develop or accept new ideas

❑ a lot ❑ somewhat ❑ not at all

c. Communicate your own ideas.

❑ a lot   ❑ somewhat   ❑ not at all

d. Understand other points of view.

❑ a lot   ❑ somewhat   ❑ not at all

e. Resolve disputes.

❑ a lot   ❑ somewhat   ❑ not at all

f. Solve problems.

❑ a lot   ❑ somewhat   ❑ not at all

g. Set and achieve group goals.

❑ a lot   ❑ somewhat   ❑ not at all

h. Other:

_____

_____

26. What techniques or ideas that you learned in the program/course have you used in your work?

_____

_____

27. Were there any problems or negative consequences of the program/ course for you or other participants?

a. Some participants seem to think they know more than their peers.

❑ yes   ❑ no

b. Some participants seem to think they know more than their
   supervisors. ❏ yes ❏ no

c. Some participants act too relaxed at work. ❏ yes ❏ no

d. Some participants act too relaxed in the community. ❏ yes ❏ no

e. Other:

_____

_____

28. How do you think we can improve the program/course?

_____

_____

_____

_____

SUPERVISOR PROGRAM EVALUATION

Dear [NAME]:

Employees under your supervision have completed [PROGRAM or COURSE NAME]. Your confidential response to this brief survey will help us assess and improve these programs, and is very much appreciated. This survey is absolutely anonymous. The record kept of your responses will not contain any identifying information about you, and no one will ever know which answers you gave.

Feel free to contact me with any questions you may have. Thank you for your assistance.

Sincerely,

[NAME, TITLE, ORGANIZATION, AND CONTACT INFORMATION]

Please provide your:

1. Gender

    a. Male

    b. Female

2. Age ____

3. Highest academic level completed

    a. some college

    b. college graduate

    c. some post-graduate

    d. MA, MS, pastoral degree, or counseling license

    e. some doctoral

    f. PhD or other doctoral degree

4. Current title or rank

    a. Sheriff's Department

        i.   Deputy

        ii.   Sergeant

        iii. Lieutenant

        iv.   Commander

        v.   Chief

        vi.   Assistant Sheriff

        vii. Under Sheriff

        viii. Sheriff

    b. Police Department

        i.   Officer

        ii.   Sergeant

    iii.   Lieutenant

    iv.   Captain

    v.   Commander

    vi.   Deputy Chief

    vii.   Assistant Chief

    viii. Chief of Police

(FOR PRIVATE SECTOR)

    i.   Hourly worker or non-exempt employee

    ii.   Salary worker or exempt employee

    iii.   Frontline manager

    iv.   Middle manager

    v.   Department head

    vi.   Executive (CFO, COO, CTO)

    vii.   CEO/President

Based on what you know or have heard about the program/course . . .

5.   Did the program/course seem different from other college classes or training programs in . . .

   a. the subject matter? ❑ yes ❑ no

   b. the teaching style? ❑ yes ❑ no

   c. participants' roles in class? ❑ yes ❑ no

6.   Did the program/course seem different from other police (FOR PRIVATE SECTOR, OMIT POLICE) training courses in . . .

   a. the subject matter? ❑ yes ❑ no

   b. the teaching style? ❑ yes ❑ no

   c. participants' roles in class? ❑ yes ❑ no

7. What do you think was unique about the program/course?

_____

_____

_____

_____

Based on what you know or have heard about the program/course . . .

8. Did you find it difficult to support or justify the program/course?

❑ very ❑ somewhat ❑ not at all

9. Did any of the participants complain about the program/course classes?

❑ a lot ❑ some ❑ none

10. If so, what program/course activities might participants have found irrelevant?

a. Working in groups ❑ yes ❑ no

b. Having participants decide course goals ❑ yes ❑ no

c. Not getting the answers from the instructor ❑ yes ❑ no

d. Having to resolve participants' various opinions ❑ yes ❑ no

e. Having to talk about inner feelings ❑ yes ❑ no

f. Other:

_____

_____

11. What program/course activities might participants have found challenging?

    a. Working in groups ❑ yes   ❑ no

    b. Having participants decide course goals ❑ yes   ❑ no

    c. Not getting the answers from the instructor ❑ yes   ❑ no

    d. Having to resolve participants' various opinions ❑ yes   ❑ no

    e. Having to talk about inner feelings ❑ yes   ❑ no

    f. Other:

    _____

    _____

12. What program/course activities might participants have found uncomfortable?

    a. Working in groups ❑ yes   ❑ no

    b. Having participants decide course goals ❑ yes   ❑ no

    c. Not getting definite answers from the instructor ❑ yes   ❑ no

    d. Having to resolve participants' various opinions ❑ yes   ❑ no

    e. Having to talk about inner feelings ❑ yes   ❑ no

    f. Other:

    _____

    _____

Based on what you know or have heard about the program/course . . .

13. Did participants seem to get more comfortable with class activities over time?

    ❑ very   ❑ somewhat   ❑ not at all

14. Did participants work like part of a team?

    ❑ very   ❑ somewhat   ❑ not at all

15. Do you think participants learned about good leadership in the program/course?

    ❑ a lot   ❑ somewhat   ❑ not at all

16. Do you think participants practiced good leadership in the program/course?

    ❑ a lot   ❑ somewhat   ❑ not at all

17. What surprised you about participants' response to the program/ course experience?

    _____

    _____

18. Did you support a participant for promotion or desired transfer?
    ❑ yes   ❑ no

19. If so, did you feel that the participant earned promotion by completing the program successfully? ❑ yes   ❑ no

20. Did you notice improved leadership skills on the part of program/ course participants? ❑ yes   ❑ no

21. In their work with others, do you feel that the program/course helped participants . . .

    a. Feel more confident in their leadership abilities.

    ❑ a lot   ❑ somewhat   ❑ not at all

b. Develop or accept new ideas.

☐ a lot   ☐ somewhat   ☐ not at all

c. Communicate their own ideas.

☐ a lot   ☐ somewhat   ☐ not at all

d. Understand other points of view.

☐ a lot   ☐ somewhat   ☐ not at all

e. Resolve disputes.

☐ a lot   ☐ somewhat   ☐ not at all

f. Solve problems.

☐ a lot   ☐ somewhat   ☐ not at all

g. Set and achieve group goals.

☐ a lot   ☐ somewhat   ☐ not at all

h. Other:

_____

_____

22. In their work with the community, do you feel that the program/ course helped participants . . .

a. Feel more confident in their leadership abilities.

☐ a lot   ☐ somewhat   ☐ not at all

b. Develop or accept new ideas.

☐ a lot   ☐ somewhat   ☐ not at all

c. Communicate their own ideas.

   ❑ a lot   ❑ somewhat   ❑ not at all

d. Understand other points of view.

   ❑ a lot   ❑ somewhat   ❑ not at all

e. Resolve disputes.

   ❑ a lot   ❑ somewhat   ❑ not at all

f. Solve problems.

   ❑ a lot   ❑ somewhat   ❑ not at all

g. Set and achieve group goals.

   ❑ a lot   ❑ somewhat   ❑ not at all

h. Other:

_____

_____

23. What new techniques, ideas, or skills learned in the program/course have participants applied in their work?

_____

_____

_____

_____

24. Based on what you have seen or heard, have there been any problems or negative consequences of the program/course?

    a. Participants seem to think they know more than their peers.

       ❑ yes   ❑ no

    b. Participants seem to think they know more than their supervisors.

       ❑ yes   ❑ no

    c. Participants act too relaxed at work.   ❑ yes   ❑ no

    d. Participants act too relaxed in the community.   ❑ yes   ❑ no

    e. Other:

    _____

    _____

25. How do you think we can improve the program/course?

    _____

    _____

    _____

    _____

Index

A

abstract conceptualization, 8–9

accountability, 11, 81, 189–190

action learning, 9

active experience, 5–6

active learning
    in facilitative learning
        environments, 30
    participant resistance to, 38–39
    relationships in, 40–44
    in self-directed learning, 10–11

active listening, 69, 188–189

active thinkers, 181

activities (See *classroom activities.*)

adaptive purposes, in groups, 51

adjourning (stage 5), 51, 67–68

adjusting group dynamics, 77–82

Adler, R., 185

adult learners, needs of, 7

adult learning, 3–24, 193–194
    critiques of, 19
    and developmental learning theory,
        3–4
    experiential learning, 8–10
    facilitation, 14–19
    factors impacting, 5–7
    group learning, 14
    instructional approaches using,
        8–18
    leadership training based on, 4–7

respect in, ix
    self-directed learning, 10–11
    transformational learning, 12–13
    and value of facilitative leadership
        training, 18–23

adult learning theory, 5–7, 105

advancement, 91, 108 (See also
    promotions.)

affective responses, 187–188

agendas, lesson, 171

aggressive participants, 55, 78, 79

aging, as factor in learning, 6

Allan, S., 33

alternative solutions, 61, 149

alumni blogs, 68

Alumni Program Evaluation
    in research design, 106
    responses to, 111–123
    survey questions, 205–212

ambiguity, role, 56

Anderson, K., 32

andragogy, 5

Apollo 13 (film), 159

application of material
    in adult learning, 6, 193–194
    alumni views of, 115–116

appreciation, 6, 18, 38, 173

approaching leadership readings
    (lesson outline), 184–185

Argote. L., 6–7

argumentative participants, 78, 79

HOW TO PURCHASE ASTD PRESS PRODUCTS

All ASTD Press titles may be purchased through ASTD's online store at **www.store.astd.org**.

ASTD Press products are available worldwide through various outlets and booksellers. In the United States and Canada, individuals may also purchase titles (print or eBook) from:

Amazon– www.amazon.com (USA); www.amazon.com (CA)
Google Play– play.google.com/store
EBSCO– www.ebscohost.com/ebooks/home

Outside the United States, English-language ASTD Press titles may be purchased through distributors (divided geographically).

United Kingdom, Continental Europe, the Middle East, North Africa, Central Asia, and Latin America:
Eurospan Group
Phone: 44.1767.604.972
Fax: 44.1767.601.640
Email: eurospan@turpin-distribution.com
Web: www.eurospanbookstore.com
For a complete list of countries serviced via Eurospan please visit www.store.astd.org or email publications@astd.org.

South Africa:
Knowledge Resources
Phone: +27(11)880-8540
Fax: +27(11)880-8700/9829
Email: mail@knowres.co.za
Web: http://www.kr.co.za
For a complete list of countries serviced via Knowledge Resources please visit www.store.astd.org or email publications@astd.org.

Nigeria:
Paradise Bookshops
Phone: 08033075133
Email: paradisebookshops@gmail.com
Website: www.paradisebookshops.com

Asia:
Cengage Learning Asia Pte. Ltd.
Email: asia.info@cengage.com
Web: www.cengageasia.com
For a complete list of countries serviced via Cengage Learning please visit www.store.astd.org or email publications@astd.org.

India:
Cengage India Pvt. Ltd.
Phone: 011 43644 1111
Fax: 011 4364 1100
Email: asia.infoindia@cengage.com

For all other countries, customers may send their publication orders directly to ASTD. Please visit: **www.store.astd.org**.